One Moment From Gone
How a Stranger's Grip Saved Us From Trafficking

Sara N Unger

Copyright © 2025 Tenacious CLE

All rights reserved.

No part of this book may be reproduced, distributed, or transmitted in any form or by any means, including photocopying, recording, or other electronic or mechanical methods, without the prior written permission of the publisher, except in the case of brief quotations used in reviews or scholarly works.

This is a true account of events as experienced by the author. Some names, identifying details, and locations have been altered or omitted to protect privacy and safety. Any resemblance to persons not directly involved is coincidental.

Published by Tenacious CLE

ISBN: 979-8-9932475-0-2

Library of Congress Control Number: 2025920489

Cover design by the author
First edition 1.2
Printed in the United States of America, Willoughby, OH

Author's Note

This memoir reflects my personal experience and opinions. Names and some identifying details in this memoir have been changed to protect privacy and safety. The events described are true to my experience; the sequence and geography reflect the day as I lived it, with minor adjustments where doing so reduces risk to bystanders and to the people whose choices intersected with mine.

The book does not make allegations against specific individuals or communities. It is intended to increase awareness of trafficking tactics and everyday prevention. No sexual violence is depicted.

If you are a traveler, know that vigilance is not paranoia; it is care. The story that follows includes moments when ordinary details meant more than they should have. I include them here because that is how danger often arrives: disguised as routine.

If you are a survivor, read only as far as your breath allows. Skip chapters. Throw the book across the room. Dog-ear what strengthens you and ignore the rest. You owe no one more pain.

If you are someone who has never felt your safety negotiated in public, I invite you to believe the people who have. When someone says, "I had a feeling," what they usually mean is: my nervous system recognized a pattern before my mind found language. The body keeps many kinds of intelligence. I am alive because another woman put her hand on mine and told me to run.

Table of Contents

AUTHOR'S NOTE 3

THE BACKGROUND 8

SIGNS ON THE ROAD 16

THE CALL 24

THE DRIVE 39

THE WAITING 48

THE TICKET 64

THE WAITING GAME 76

THE INTERROGATION 83

THE VAN 91

THE WARNING 105

THE RETURN 118

THE ESCAPE 131

THE ESCAPE INSTRUCTIONS & DRIVE 142

THE AFTERMATH 152

THE TELLING 166

SILENCE & TRANSFORMATION 173

CHOOSING LIFE 179

RESOURCES & SAFETY 184

STAY CONNECTED 185

PROFESSIONAL DISCLAIMER 186

AFTERWORD 187

ACKNOWLEDGMENTS 188

NOTES & FURTHER READING 189

READING GROUP & CLASSROOM QUESTIONS 190

ABOUT THE AUTHOR 192

HOW TO USE & SHARE THIS BOOK 193

Her grip was sudden, firm.

*"**Don't move**," she whispered, her voice low but urgent. "**See that van? They're going to snatch us.**"*

Chapter 1

The Background

I have been traveling alone for years. Each spring, I take a week for myself, a ritual I've kept for at least a decade. These trips are my reset, a time to step outside the noise of my everyday life and remember who I am when I'm not pulled in a dozen directions.

For me, solo travel is a kind of ceremony. A week of serenity in mostly silence, hiking, reflecting, letting the stress and static of daily obligations melt away. Carefree and excited, I always look forward to setting my own schedule, following my own rhythm.

My first stop is always the same: a grocery store. There's something almost sacred about that first walk through the aisles. The hum of the refrigerators, the smell of coffee beans from the grinder, the faint chill of the produce section, it all feels like the true beginning of the trip. I load the passenger seat with granola bars, oatmeal, fruit leathers, dried fruit, water, and plenty of caffeine. Each item has its place, lined up within arm's reach. It's my travel survival kit, close enough to grab without breaking the rhythm of the road.

By the time I pull back onto the highway, the drive has already become my sanctuary, music shuffled endlessly as I sing until my throat is sore and watch the horizon roll by like a living painting.

When I travel, I'm searching for peace, quiet, silence, the kind of serenity you can't find in daily life. A few years ago in Sedona, I pulled off onto a side road and followed a small trail up to a hill. The sky was heavy with enormous, rolling grey clouds, huge and fluffy, like brushstrokes smeared across a vast canvas. They weren't threatening, just powerful, a reminder of how small I was in their shadow. I sat there for hours, camera in hand, capturing angles and light. One of those photographs still hangs framed on my wall. I look at it often, not for its technical quality, but for what it reminds me of: how alive I felt in that moment, how quiet my soul became under that sky.

Before this trip, I had just purchased a refurbished camera and a used lens, determined to teach myself how to photograph the night sky. My first attempt had been in my backyard, and it was a disaster: too much exposure, the ISO set wrong, the moon too bright and uncooperative. The pictures were all washed out, a blur of mistakes. But I stayed outside for hours, fingers numb, tweaking settings until finally, one frame came back clear. Not perfect, but mine. It felt like conquering a mountain no one else could see.

For the first time, I wasn't relying on automatic settings or someone else's instructions. I had figured it out myself. That sense of accomplishment carried me forward into this trip like fuel.

I wanted this journey to be about more than hiking. I wanted to give myself space to explore the art of star photography, to stand in the stillness of dark skies and let my camera capture what my eyes alone could not. After weeks of research on my iPad late at night, I booked time in three "dark sky" destinations, places where city lights wouldn't wash out the brilliance overhead. I pictured myself standing on balconies wrapped in blankets, camera steady on its tripod, waiting for the Milky Way to emerge in long, slow swirls of light. Sedona and Springdale had been my favorites before, but this third destination had me buzzing with anticipation. It was a hotel built with photographers in mind; balconies designed for long nights of shooting, a place where even silence felt curated for stargazers. I remember texting a friend who had been helping me troubleshoot settings, telling him I had found the jackpot.

Not everything I planned was about the stars. I had also booked a tour with a local company, thinking it would be another way to experience the land without the pressure of navigating it myself. Adventure and relaxation, that was what I expected. A chance to learn the history of the land while supporting local small businesses, something I've always cared about deeply. Small businesses are dreams turned tangible, built with someone's time, heart, and determination. I take pride in contributing to that; whether it's a roadside stand, a handmade candle back home, or a guided tour in a faraway place. At the time, this decision felt like one more thoughtful detail in a carefully planned trip.

I did not start traveling alone because I was brave; I started because I was tired of asking permission to breathe. A decade ago, I promised myself a few days each year that belonged only to me, no schedules, no working, no apologizing for silence. I called it a reset because that sounded responsible, but it was something simpler: a remembering.

The first year I booked a different city each night and ate supermarket food on a balcony that overlooked a parking lot. I watched clouds and wrote down three things a day I could not name at home: the way dusk smells after heat, the color of shadow on red rock, how quiet can feel like company. The next year I hiked farther, drove longer, learned the names of stars I could not see in my city. A few days were not enough; I stretched the ritual to a full week. After seven days of being unobserved, I returned more wholly to the people I loved. I listened better. I hurried less. I stopped mistaking depletion for virtue.

Some years the week was nothing but weather and walking; other years it was a conversation with a stranger who handed me a map and told me which trail gets the best view of the sunset. Every year I refined the ritual: snacks in the passenger seat, playlists that held memories like pressed flowers, a camera that asked me to look more than speak. The ritual made me attentive. Attentive felt safer, or so I believed.

Rituals don't prevent storms; they help you stand inside one long enough to decide what to do next. This year I came for stars and quiet, and I would leave with a different kind of instruction, the first step in a chain of events that would shift the entire journey and leave me carrying something far heavier than the camera on my shoulder, something I would never be able to set down.

Chapter 2

Signs on the Road

The morning of that day, I headed east. The highway stretched flat and wide in front of me, the kind of road that feels endless, with nothing but open sky pressing down on either side. The world felt washed clean after the storm, the horizon sharp against the pale blue morning. There weren't many other travelers, just me and a scattering of vehicles far in the distance, each one swallowed quickly by the expanse. The snow that had fallen the day before had melted from the asphalt, but white patches clung stubbornly to fields and fence lines, reminders of how rare storms like this were here.

It didn't take long before the billboards started appearing. At first, they were a blur, just flashes of lettering against the open land. Then another. And another. By the fifth or sixth I finally slowed my glance enough to read: **HUMAN TRAFFICKING HAPPENS HERE TOO.** A photo of a young girl. A phone number. The words were plain, almost bureaucratic, black on white, more public notice than movie poster. In just over a hundred miles, I counted thirty, maybe forty. Why here? Why this road? Each time the message appeared it burrowed a little deeper, unsettling in its repetition. I tightened my hands on the wheel and tucked the thought away. The park was waiting.

When I arrived, the national park looked transformed beneath a fresh dusting of snow. Powder clung to ledges and fallen logs, soft and clean, reshaping the otherworldly landscape into something rare. Instead of the vivid reds I'd seen in other parks, this place held muted purples, silvers, and browns; tones that shifted with the light and made the petrified wood glow as if fossilized mid-breath. The air was crisp in the 50s, the kind of chill that wakes you up without biting too hard. I drew long, deliberate breaths just to feel the cold move through me. My boots crunched where snow lingered; in other stretches the path was bare and dry. The quiet was deep. In most places I was alone, one of the gifts of traveling off-season.

The land felt endless, layers of sediment cut into knife-sharp lines that banded the hills. I found myself tracing those lines with my eyes and wondering what each layer was made of. I meant to ask at the visitor center and forgot. Around each turn the colors shifted, some slopes white-laced, others clean and dark, like the landscape was turning pages on its own history.

I wandered for hours, camera in hand, collecting contrasts: snow against stone, pale sky against ancient trunks. Dogs padded by with tails wagging, their owners offering quick smiles. I paused to stage my Danny DeVito doll, a small six-inch crocheted version of my favorite actor, against the backdrop. A woman laughed and introduced her dog, Harry Pawter, and for a moment the oddness of the morning softened into simple shared silliness. Someone once told me weather makes the best pictures. That day, I believed it.

On impulse I pulled into a roadside shop. The smell met me at the door, musty, mothball-heavy, the scent of old trunks and forgotten corners. It lifted my great-grandparents' attic into the room, dust and discovery braided together. I asked the woman at the counter about the billboards; she blinked, confused, and shook her head. No idea.

My next stop was a tiny city I'd only ever known from a song. Driving in, I half expected disappointment, and at first, I was right: tired streets, paint peeling from storefronts. But at the famous corner under a sun-bleached street sign, the air shifted. A traveler stepped up with a guitar, strummed, and launched into the whole song. I thought it would feel hokey. It didn't. A small crowd gathered; people clapped, laughed. When he hit the lyric that made the place a cliché, strangers lifted the chorus as if we'd practiced. I joined full-voiced, unembarrassed, recording a few seconds as people danced. For a moment it felt like we'd known one another for years, a warm pocket of joy stitched into the day.

Inside the shops I asked again about the billboards. More shrugs. I purchased a few items for my mom and dad and then I got back in the car and kept drifting town to town until a highway billboard shouted in block letters: **YOU FOUND IT.** *Found what?* I thought, easing off at the exit. The place turned out to be more slogan than substance, quiet streets, souvenir rooms that felt like time capsules: cedar and folded fabric, everything paused. Inside the shops I asked again about the trafficking billboards. More shrugs. At my third stop the woman hesitated and called for her husband. He leaned in and lowered his voice: he'd heard something. A few girls, some children, gone missing from smaller, more isolated towns. He wasn't sure it was true, only that people whispered. I drove away unsettled, the rhythm of the day slightly off.

That evening, I ate at a restaurant with "Bigfoot" in the name, imagining kitsch, maybe a mural looming over red vinyl booths. Instead, I walked into a dim mall food court. The food was forgettable; the seat was mine alone. There was a time when eating alone had terrified me, exposure, vulnerability, the sense of being observed. Two memories pulsed up: footsteps quickening behind me to match my pace; a hand gripping my waist on a crowded dance floor, dragging me toward an exit while my body froze. Over the years I worked to reclaim it. Eating alone became a small act of defiance, of freedom. Tonight, the fear's edges had softened.

I was tired from the day but content. Snow, photographs, small towns, laughter; it had added up to something good. I thought the night would end that way. Maybe I'd brave a few night shots despite the cold.

Then my phone rang.

The screen lit without meaning. I swiped. A voice: "May I speak to Sara?"

Fluorescent lights hummed overhead. Nirvana leaked from a speaker somewhere behind me. Footsteps passed and faded; no one sat near my table. I answered, expecting nothing. The voice continued, even and ordinary, the way voices do before they change the temperature of a room.

I didn't know yet that this call would pull me out of the day and set me on the edge of something far darker.

Chapter 3

The Call

I was still sitting at the table, half-distracted by the music overhead. Nirvana drifted through the otherwise empty restaurant, Kurt Cobain's voice echoing off bright lights and laminate tables. For a Friday night, the place felt abandoned. The hum of the soda machine and a faint clatter from the kitchen filled more space than the handful of staff who drifted in and out.

I'd chosen a table off to the side, away from the windows, where I could watch the entrance without being obvious. In front of me: a half-eaten plate of food that looked better on the menu than it did in front of me. The name of the restaurant had promised charm. Fluorescents offered reality.

My phone rang.

"May I speak to Sara?"

The voice was cheerful, exactly what I'd expect from a tour company. Friendly. Upbeat. The cadence of someone whose job is to make strangers feel welcome. She introduced herself quickly and said she was calling about my booking; the tone was breezy, practiced, almost glossy.

"Could you do eight a.m. tomorrow?"

I told her I wouldn't be in the area until noon or one; the drive was too long. A beat.

"Could you make it by eleven?"

Again, no. I repeated my timeline. The facts were simple.

Then she asked, "Are you a single traveler?"

The first time, it felt like a form field. Check a box, move along. I'd heard variations of it in Sedona, in

Springdale, places where being one person somehow turns you into a problem to solve. Mild annoyance rose, then I let it go.

She tried again on the schedule; noncommittal, circling and then: "Are you a single traveler?"

The second time, the question landed differently. The words were the same; the temperature wasn't. I sat a little straighter without meaning to, as if posture could sharpen hearing.

We went around the schedule once more. She offered a vague *maybe the day after*, a blur of options that somehow never became an option. And then:

"Are you a single traveler?"

The third time, something in my gut tipped. The tone had shifted; too clean, too performed the way bad acting sits wrong even when you can't say why. Her cheer didn't match her words. It glossed over something I suddenly wanted a handhold for.

What 'normal' sounds like is easy to recognize if you've heard it enough.

In Sedona a year earlier, I'd booked a sunset tour as a party of one. The woman on the phone had sounded tired in the honest way of someone at the end of a long day. She didn't ask if I was alone; she asked if I would mind sitting in the front seat since I was a solo booking. I told her I didn't mind as I get car sick sometimes and I usually don't in the front passenger seat. She told me to bring water, warned me about dust, and said the driver liked to stop where the light hits the buttes sideways. When I apologized for being the last seat, she laughed, *we love solo travelers; they're never late*, and then repeated the meet-up spot twice, slowly, so I could write it down. The tone matched the content. Everything felt ordinary.

In Kanab once, a clerk glanced at my single reservation and said, *You want quiet? Take room 214; it's far from the ice machine.* No curiosity, no fishing. A small kindness disguised as logistics.

Those calls had made me feel like a customer. This one made me feel like a category.

I kept testing the memory as if I could prove myself wrong. Maybe I was overreacting. Maybe this was just a new hire reading from a script. Maybe the question had to be asked for insurance or head counts or the company's version of safety. *But then why ask it three times?* If it were a form field, it would have stayed checked.

Heat rose in my face. The billboards from the morning surfaced without my permission: **HUMAN TRAFFICKING HAPPENS HERE TOO** the black type, the girl's photograph, the number. Thirty, maybe forty of them in a hundred miles. I had tucked them away then. They untucked themselves now.

I tried to lock something down; date, time, a detail that would make this ordinary. She didn't. My mind began its quiet calculus: If this is fine, why does it feel wrong? If it's wrong, what's my next safe step? Behind me the music shifted; the speaker popped; plates clinked in the kitchen like wind chimes in a draft.

We ended the call with nothing settled.

I didn't text anyone. Didn't post. I sat and watched my fingers drum against the table as if they belonged to someone else. It's strange what the body chooses when it can't choose certainty: tap, stop, tap again. My thoughts circled the repetition; once, twice, three times and the way her tone had sat too bright on top of it.

I told myself to shake it off. That it was nothing. But words don't echo unless they have walls to bounce off.

Fluorescent hum. Mop water. A teenager sweeping circles in the food court. Somewhere, Nirvana gave way to a different song I couldn't name. I stood because standing seemed like the next right thing. I threw away my tray and missed the bin by an inch, then corrected it, order as proof that I still controlled something.

In the bathroom I locked a stall and watched my breath: in for four, hold for four, out for six. Old skills, automatic. My face looked ordinary in the mirror, which felt like a small betrayal. Water gave me an excuse to linger.

I zipped my jacket; the temperature outside had dropped to twenty-eight and slung my bag over my shoulder. I slid Danny into the bag the way I always do, a small ritual that calms me. He'd flown out with me in his own seat, swaddled in a Browns pillow and blanket; strangers had laughed and taken pictures at CLE. Now he was tucked away, and even that felt like part of staying safe.

Outside, the cold air cut clean across my face. The street was quiet; my boots made the only sound I could hear. But her words carried louder than the night.

Single traveler.

Alone.

Just one.

In the parking lot the air smelled like cold and oil. My car blinked; I sat with my palms at ten and two and narrated my way into motion the way you talk a frightened child through a doorway.

Turn right.

Merge now.

Breathe. You're okay. You're okay. You're okay.

The night had gone glossy, reflections and glare. Streetlights stretched the road like taffy. The rearview mirror turned into a rule.

In the car I built an option tree because trees are steadier than feelings.

Branch one: keep the booking.

Assume incompetence, not malice. Show up late morning as planned. Downsides: I arrive tired from the drive; I'm a known single traveler; if something feels off on arrival, options shrink quickly.

Branch two: reschedule with boundaries.

Call back in the morning and set terms out loud: public meet-up point, confirm guide's name and vehicle description. If the tone shifts again, I cancel. Downsides: I am still the person who made the call; my number is still in their phone.

Branch three: cancel now.

Email only. Leave a paper trail. Book a different experience with a company that publishes driver names and plate numbers or skip the tour entirely. Downsides: I lose the story I thought I was going to have. I disappoint no one but myself and still feel disappointed.

Branch four: triangulate.

Ask the hotel front desk whether they know the

company. Ask a ranger, if the park is open early, whether they've heard of them. Ask a shopkeeper who has watched the corner longer than any website has existed. Local knowledge is usually plainer than marketing copy.

Branch five: change the field.
Leave earlier than planned tomorrow. Different route. Different town for coffee. Shift the timing of everything by a few hours so no one's expectations can stick to my day.

The tree did not tell me what to do, but it reminded me that choice still existed. Dread likes to pretend you have only one option, walk straight into it. I kept adding small rules I could live by in the morning: don't answer numbers I don't recognize; meet in public with exits behind me; if even one unfixable detail feels wrong, I go.

Upstairs I wrote the rules on a sticky note because handwriting can make thought feel real. I placed it under the room phone as if proximity might help. Then I laid out the next day in practical pieces: gas, weather, the map that would keep me on larger roads. I set the alarm twice. Packed the bag so the things I'd want fastest were closest to my hand. When I turned off the light the room didn't get darker; it got louder; the heater's cough, plumbing somewhere in the walls, the periodic blink of the smoke detector like the heartbeat of the building.

I told myself a sentence I use in sessions with other people and sometimes forget to offer myself: *You don't have to decide everything tonight. You only have to decide the next right thing.*

Before bed, I did the usual inventory; locks, latch, peephole and added new steps: leave the bathroom light on; check the balcony latch twice. Backpack within reach. Shoes lined by the door, toes out, as if speed depended on alignment.

Sleep did not come. I lay still and traced the voice that had found me in a food court states away from home, the ordinary opening line, *May I speak to Sara?*, and the way ordinary can tilt without warning. After midnight the heater coughed; I startled like the building had spoken. I turned my phone off, on, off again. Opened my camera settings; closed them. Counted breaths. Watched the red dot on the smoke detector blink itself through the dark.

Morning would ask for calls and choices and the vocabulary of aftermath. For now, I practiced moving through small, safe tasks: boil water, make tea, hold the mug with both hands. Ceramic steadies more than you'd think. Outside, the sky lightened by degrees.

Inside, I gave myself the truth in pieces: you are here; you are breathing; more will be asked of you; you will answer.

Chapter 4

The Drive

By morning, the snow had melted. The ground was dry and crisp, as though the storm had never happened. The air carried that cool, refreshing feel of early spring, light-jacket weather, in the fifties. I stood outside the hotel room and breathed deeper just to taste it, each inhale a quiet reminder that I was alive and on my own terms.

I did my usual check before leaving wallet, keys, phone; camera batteries full; lens cloth in the side pocket; water bottles within reach. I opened the curtains and let the room return to ordinary. It felt like a small ceremony of un-guarding.

Crossing a state line, I pulled over for my ritual. Blue, white, and brownish-orange letters marked the welcome sign, bold against an unbroken sky. I held Danny up and snapped his picture in his fifteenth state. He was ridiculous and perfect, a thread stitched through these trips, proof that I could carry humor as well as caution. A couple of drivers honked in encouragement; one gave a thumbs-up out the window. I laughed, surprised by how easy it felt to be visible again.

A car of college girls swung in beside me, doors flying open, laughter bright as coins hitting a tabletop. "Will you take one of us?" one called, cheeks wind-pinked, hair lifting in the breeze. I framed them under the big sky, counted down, and handed the phone back; they insisted on taking mine, too, and I let myself grin the way I only do on the road. "We just stopped at a spot from *Forrest Gump*," another said, eyes shining. The idea caught like a burr in wool, small, then impossible to ignore. After they pulled away, music low and windows down, I decided I needed to add that as one of my photography spots for the day, too.

I'm a minimalist about stops. On solo trips I plan my fluids, sip sparingly, and only stop for gas. Fewer variables, fewer chances to end up in the wrong place at the wrong time. Out here, towns sit far apart like islands, so I decided to return to a station I'd used before. I knew that once I rounded the bend the sign would tilt into view, the green dinosaur lifting its cheerful neck over the road. Familiarity is a kind of safety. I pulled in.

The pump handles were sun-faded; the concrete held the dark halos of a thousand fill-ups. I set the nozzle and scanned the lot the way I always do who's here, who's watching, who's leaving. Inside, the clerk sat behind glass, counting bills; a bulletin board near the door offered the usual local collage, lost dog, pancake breakfast, softball sign-ups. Ordinary notices tacked up with pins, their corners softened by hands. The attendant asked where I was headed. "North," I said, and he nodded as though north were a personality trait. I bought a sleeve of peanut-butter crackers, tucked them into the passenger-seat lineup. I paid with a card, kept my phone face-down in my palm, and returned to the car without lingering. The tank capped, the doors locked, the route set. Back on the highway.

The first pull-off for the movie view wasn't right. The angle felt wrong; the horizon didn't match the frame in my head. I drove farther, the road bending between buttes until the lines aligned. I parked, stepped out, and felt that click a photographer waits for, the world arranging itself into composition and inviting you to press the shutter. For a minute I stood there not as a tourist, or a woman traveling alone, but as one of the many who had paused in that exact place to catch a memory as it went by.

The drive turned to backroads, two-lane ribbons threading wide country. Not jagged peaks but buttes: broad, flat-topped giants carved by time, their orange-red faces catching light and holding it like warmth. I rolled the windows down and let the car fill with air. Dust, a hint of sage, sun on upholstery. I turned the volume up and sang.

For some reason I put "Life Is a Highway" on repeat. It's a song that usually annoys me; overplayed, too obvious but the chorus matched the day's forward lean. Between repeats the shuffle offered a few strays that felt like notes to self: a line about keeping your eyes on the road and your hands upon the wheel, another about running down a dream that won't let you go. Lyrics have a way of sounding like instructions when you're alone for miles.

At a turnout a man glanced my way with an expression I translated as judgment, maybe impatience, one of those looks whose meaning changes with your mood. The old defensiveness flared and, absurdly, my brain offered, *I'll egg you, jerk*. The thought startled a laugh out of me. I shook my head, slid back into the driver's seat, and the laugh remained. Nothing could dent the day.

By then the unease from the phone call had thinned to a watercolor wash. The words that had echoed, *single traveler, alone, just one*, had dissolved the way snow disappears by noon: not gone exactly, just absorbed into everything else. My ADHD works that way. What is urgent one day can slip behind a brighter object the next. Attention is a loyal dog until it spots a rabbit.

I told myself this was perspective, not denial. I rehearsed the reasonable story, new hire, clumsy script, nothing sinister, and let the road carry me forward. The music helped. So did motion. If anxiety is an animal that circles, a highway is a long, straight gaze that keeps it from tightening the loop.

The buttes grew larger as the road narrowed. Heat shimmered above the shoulder. A roadside sign warned of open range; a mile later a hand-painted board offered CASH FOR CARS with a number nailed on crookedly; then another official marker I barely registered at the time: NO SERVICES NEXT 50 MILES. None of it meant anything in the moment, just scenery, just text, yet later those signs would replay in my mind as if they'd been narrating.

When I pulled into an overlook, the wind pressed steady at my back, and for a moment I closed my eyes and stood there, feet firm, letting the pressure hold me up. It felt like a blessing and I accepted it as one.

A few small things happened that I did not put together until later: a white truck that appeared twice, first in the rearview, then ahead at the next turnout; a second car that lingered at a distance and then fell away; a text from an unknown number I ignored because I had decided to ignore unknowns. None of it registered as pattern. That is the nature of peace, it makes you generous with coincidence.

I drove on. I sang. I told myself I was fine. The sky widened and widened and then widened again.

I did not know it then, but the relief I felt was a kind of false weather, clear, warming, easy to believe in. The kind that makes you take off your jacket right before the wind changes.

Chapter 5

The Waiting

When I finally reached the hotel, I called the tour office. No one answered. I left a message, keeping my tone polite even as irritation pressed at the edges of my voice.

"Hi, I made it to the hotel. I haven't heard back from anyone and wanted to confirm what time I should be there today. Please let me know."

The area felt so remote I wasn't even sure my call had gone through, so I followed with an email. My fingers hovered over Send longer than usual, rereading the lines, sanding them smooth so they sounded calm and reasonable. When I hit the button, the screen sat still, no confirmation, no reassuring chime. Just silence.

I checked the bar of service out of habit, one pale line clinging to the corner of the screen like a last polite guest. I waited the ritual ten seconds, then the superstitious ten more, and refreshed my inbox. Nothing. The remoteness felt physical, not just a map fact but a room I'd entered: fewer people, fewer signals, fewer second chances. I toggled airplane mode on and off, the tech equivalent of knocking and then knocking again.

My calendar still showed the original booking. I stared at the time-stamp as if it could testify for me in the hours ahead. The ER taught me to love time-stamps; they make stories linear when memory tries to go sideways. I copied the confirmation number into a notes app and screen-shotted the page, a small way of saying: I was here, and I asked in good faith.

Outside, wind lifted dust into low swirls across the pavement. A truck coughed, idled, moved on. I told myself the silence was just logistics; thin staffing, poor reception, the way weekends make people casual. Still, the quiet pressed back like a door that won't open all the way: enough space to squeeze through if you insist, not enough to feel welcome.

Inside, the front-desk clerk greeted me with a careful smile. Her words landed heavy: my room wasn't ready yet. No paperwork. No key. A shrug, a suggestion to come back later. On most days I would have brushed it off, I was hours early, but in that moment, it lodged like grit in a shoe. I was here, but not quite welcome. Close, but without a place to set my things.

"Check-in is at four," she said, kind but immovable.

"I understand," I answered, matching her tone. "If anything opens earlier, would you mind calling?" I slid my number across the counter as if numbers could make space sooner.

She nodded and stapled it to a square of paper I never saw again. A small bell chimed when the door opened behind me; a family shuffled in with the tired choreography of arrivals, plastic bags, a child asleep on a shoulder, a cooler thumping against a shin. I stepped aside and let them pass, the way you do when your day has become waiting.

I set a quiet boundary in my head: I don't sit in lobbies to be watched. If I'm going to wait, I'll wait on my own terms, moving, looking, choosing where my back goes. It wasn't anger; it was an old rule that keeps my nervous system from overheating. The lobby light was beautiful, wide windows, desert in every pane, but beauty does not always mean safety. I walked toward the gift shop because shelves are easier than chairs.

I drifted into the gift shop to pass time. The space was dated but warm, every shelf touched by someone's hands. Cedar hung in the air. Windows wrapped the lobby in glass so the desert kept you company: wide, quiet, patched with snow that clung where the sun could not reach. I lingered at the magnet display, fingers over glossy fragments of the landscape. Weeks earlier, a family member had dropped a stone magnet from this place. It broke, glued back together with apologetic hands. I'd shrugged; said it didn't matter. Standing here, the memory felt like a tiny omen I did not believe in and could not quite ignore. I slipped a replacement into my basket as if paying a debt I hadn't named. Postcards for my grandma too, she saved every one.

    The postcards were the old-fashioned kind with glossy fronts and backs that took ink well. I always choose a pen that doesn't bleed and print the address like I'm writing it for a future historian who has to make sense of our lives from paper. My grandma reads every postcard at the kitchen table, tracing the sentences with a finger as if underlining matters, then tucks them into a box already full of other places I've stood. It comforts me to imagine a record that doesn't live on a server farm but in a cardboard archive that smells faintly of soap and her favorite perfume, Wind Song.

    The magnet wall held scenes I'd already tried to catch with my camera: a slab of petrified wood lit like amber from within; a road ribboning toward buttes; a winter photograph with snow lodged in shadows the sun couldn't touch. The replacement clicked against the metal backer with that small, satisfying sound of things finding where they belong. I told myself it was nothing, just a souvenir. But I have learned to notice when my hands reach for symbols without asking my head's permission. The broken one at home. The new one here. A ledger even if I pretended not to be balancing it.

I added a small notebook near the register, palm-sized, elastic band, pages that could take pressure without tearing. Not everything belongs in a phone. Some notes feel safer on paper. The cashier wrapped my items with deliberate care, like protecting fragile pieces of me I hadn't realized were there.

After checkout I tucked the bag in my car and walked the property. Behind the hotel, snow crystals caught the morning light, bright as ground glass. I raised my camera for ordinary frames that still managed to soothe. Breathing in the cold, I let the exhale lengthen. For a moment, unease loosened.

My phone did not. No missed call. No voicemail. No reply. The tour was meant to be today; the silence tightened like a hand at my elbow.

I sat at a wooden picnic table near the lot. The boards were cold beneath my legs. From there I could see both the open desert and the small choreography of arrival: children angling toward the restrooms, parents corralling them with tired voices, couples pausing for quick photos before trucks swallowed them. Their laughter floated around me like a language I could not quite join.

I made the table into a tiny command post. Phone face-down so I wouldn't keep refreshing; keys where my right hand would find them without looking; bag strap looped around my ankle, not because I expected theft but because habits travel with you. A ranger truck rolled past and parked nose-out. I liked the geometry of that; quick exit baked into the angle.

A father took a photo of his family and said, "One more, just in case," and the teenager groaned the way teenagers everywhere groan when living people insist on memories. A woman in a sunhat tried to fold a map back into the shape it had when it was new and failed with grace. Two friends compared sunscreen like sommeliers tasting notes. I wrote three rules in the notebook because writing calms the part of me that wants to pace:

1. **Do not go where your body says no.**
2. **Public, visible, exits behind you.**
3. **If it gets vague, ask concrete questions out loud.**

A message from home about the Browns slid through as if football could travel where tour confirmations could not. I answered with an emoji and saved my words for later. I checked the time against the length of the drive I'd planned; the math said I still had space for the original booking if someone would only say words into a phone.

I watched the entrance and thought about how many nights in the ER started like this, waiting for the thing that would define the night to announce itself, trying to stay useful without burning energy you might need later. You learn to love the ordinary in those jobs: coffee that is reliably bad, pens that reliably disappear, the way a hallway hum tells you a shift is happening. Here the ordinary was children asking for snacks and a trash can clacking shut. I let them be the hallway for a few minutes. It helped.

A text from a friend slid through, hers always seemed to find a path. Then another family message about the Browns signing a new receiver. This one was worth responding to. Sports are a big part of my life; one of my languages, as steadying to me as a horizon line. The ordinary steadied me: evidence that the world was still normal somewhere, and that I was still tethered to it.

Across the lot, I noticed it.

The trailer.

Plain white, parked squarely in the center, two small windows cut into the side. People approached in ones and twos, glanced at a laminated sheet, handed over cash. The person inside pointed them to another person, who sent them toward the open-air trucks lined along the trailhead.

No company name. No logo. The laminated sheet listed a handful of tour offerings in neat black type, durations, a few landmarks, prices in crisp numerals, with a folded map taped behind it. No branding. No signage. Not official in any way I had expected "official" to look.

I tried to imagine how I would explain this to someone later if explaining were required. *There was a trailer,* I would say, and that would sound harmless. *There were families,* I would add, and that would sound safe. *There were trucks, and laughter.* All true. The mind wants to build verdicts from visible pieces. I took a photo of the parking lot without aiming at anything in particular, just a landscape of ordinary. It felt like setting a pin on a map I might want to find again.

A gust lifted the corner of the laminated sheet and smacked it back against the metal with a quick, hollow click. The person inside tore a receipt with a practiced wrist and handed it through the slot to a woman in a red jacket. The woman tucked it away and didn't look at it again. I noticed how quickly paper becomes pocket becomes nothing.

I stayed where I was and watched. The pattern set in like a heartbeat: cash across the sill, the soft tear of a receipt, a quick nod, a gesture toward the trucks. Diesel idled low, elastic, underscoring laughter and small talk. Dust puffed around tires; sun flashed on metal rails; a child hopped on one foot while a parent tugged at a hat strap. Each time a truck rolled forward, another group flowed into place and the rhythm re-formed.

I watched long enough to memorize it. I told myself I was just taking notes. I told myself I was being prudent. But the longer I waited for my phone to light, the closer the quiet came. My original booking lived nowhere except in my inbox and hope.

I promised myself one small test before I moved: I would sit for the length of a song and see if my phone lit. It didn't. I took a slow breath in for four, held for four, and let it out for six, the piloted exhale you learn when adrenaline is auditioning to drive.

I checked the angle of the sun and the length of the shadow my table threw across the concrete. The shadow reached almost to the first truck; if I walked now, I would step through shade into light in three strides. I prefer to move in light when making decisions. It's not magic. It's a way to give your senses the most information at once.

It never lit.

I folded the notebook shut and slipped it into the bag. I stood, brushed grit from my palms, and turned toward the trailer-that-was-a-ticket-booth. My chest tightened as I crossed the lot, nothing dramatic, just the steady cinch of a belt. It's fine, I told myself. It's just a ticket booth. The sentence sounded reasonable. My body did not believe me. My stomach coiled as if it already understood what my mind refused to say aloud.

What I didn't realize then was that this moment, this choice to keep moving forward, would become the first step into the narrow corridor where everything that followed would happen. I was already in it. I just hadn't felt the walls yet.

Chapter 6

The Ticket

Up close, the trailer felt even more temporary. No sign. No logo. Just a laminated sheet with tour options and, taped behind it, a map.

The woman at the window greeted me warmly. Sun-worn face, kind eyes, a light grey zip-up hoodie over jeans and tennis shoes. Her smile was easy, her voice the practiced calm of someone who sells reassurance for a living. She slid the laminated sheet toward me and talked through the options. The page looked professional, clean type, small photos of landmarks, exactly the kind of presentation meant to make your body believe what your mind has not checked.

What reassured me, I realized, wasn't the information; it was the format. Clean fonts imply systems. Laminated pages imply repetition. The ER taught me that packaging can borrow the authority of a hospital chart without offering the substance inside it. I looked for the small tells I'd learned to trust spelling errors, mismatched prices, a date that didn't fit the season. Nothing obvious. The map behind the sheet was real enough to be convincing and general enough to be meaningless. If you squinted, it could have been anywhere.

Her patter was soothing in the way of people who do this all day. Not pushy, just confident that you would say yes. I counted breaths and let her sentences roll over me. Somewhere behind us a child tried to whistle and made the soft, breathy almost-sound that comes just before the first real note. It was oddly tender, and for a second, I let that tenderness stand in for evidence.

My own rules clicked through: Ask one verifying question. "How many groups out today?" I asked, casual. She answered quickly "Steady" a word that could mean anything. Ask for a concrete: "Where's the meeting spot?" She tapped the counter between us. "Right back here." Vague again. My body noticed; my brain filed it under *monitor*.

   I told myself that ninety minutes was a small commitment, a hedge against the silence from the other company. Two tours if it worked out, a single story if it didn't. I heard myself agree and watched my hand accept the receipt even as another part of me kept its distance, like a nurse observing a procedure from the doorway, ready to step in if something turned.

   I chose the ninety-minute tour. The logic was simple: if the other company ever called me back, I'd still have time to do both.

   She nodded. "Ninety minutes. Good choice." Cash only. She pulled a small, handheld receipt book from the ledge and wrote quickly 90-minute tour, the price, and a start time, then tore off the slip and handed it to me. "You'll bring this back to board," she said, tapping the paper. "We'll collect it then."

At the time, it felt routine. Later I would understand what it removed: no digital trail, and once the receipt left my hand, no proof I had ever stood there.

Cash made sense in one way, remoteness simplifies systems; card readers hate dead zones. But cash also erases footprints. I tested the thought against the scene: laminated sheet for durability, map for plausibility, receipt book for the ritual of legitimacy. A line can look like a process when all it is is a line.

At the same time, it struck me as odd. Since 2020, so many places had shifted away from cash "touchless" payments, QR menus, card-only counters that the sight of cash-only beside lingering "COVID precautions" signage felt like a mismatch. If you're still invoking pandemic protocols, wouldn't contactless make more sense than bills and coins? It wasn't proof of anything; it was the kind of detail the brain files under *incongruent*. I noted the contradiction and let it sit next to the other small tells, laminated pages, a generic map, receipt slips that turned into pockets and then into nothing.

Something subtler snagged. In passing, almost as an aside, she mentioned that I was on my own and that I'd been waiting on another tour. I hadn't said a word about either. The thought flickered, maybe she'd seen me at the picnic table, maybe she was just good at reading people. I let the flicker pass.

She looked over my shoulder and called, bright and practiced, "**Joe, here's one for you.**"

He was already near the trailer. The moment our eyes met, a chill slid through me. He didn't smile. Didn't soften. The stare was intent and vacant at once, the look I used to see on patients under the influence when I worked in the Emergency Department: sharp, but somehow not attached to the present.

He wore a thick flannel, unbuttoned over a white T-shirt; worn jeans; boots; a hat pulled low. On the surface: local guide. In the body: something off. His stance had a heaviness to it, a slight sway that made me wonder how he handled one of the large vehicles idling nearby.

He jerked his chin: follow.

I let him take the lead and gave myself an option tree to keep panic from deciding for me.

Branch A: Routine. He's a normal guide; the trucks are full so he's staging near the huts. I cooperate, stay pleasant, keep the distance of two arm lengths, and watch for the ordinary signs: a safety speech, a clipboard, the practiced choreography of moving people.

Branch B: Vague but fixable. If details stay fuzzy, meeting point drifts, timing slips I ask very specific questions out loud. I repeat the answer back so other ears catch it. I set a boundary in a sentence: *I meet only at the trailer in view of others.* If it can't be honored, I abort.

Branch C: Hard no. If my options narrow, if I'm asked to step where I can't be seen, hand over something I don't want to surrender, or wait in a place that makes my spine light up I walk away. I don't explain. I don't apologize. Leaving is an option. People forget that.

I checked the small things I could still choose receipt tucked so I could grab it fast, phone unlocked in my hand, bag cross-body with the zipper facing in. A text hung unsent; reception hiccupped and spun. Wind lifted dust across my boots. Somewhere metal ticked in the sun. Behind us, a burst of laughter rose and fell, proof that other stories were proceeding as planned.

As we neared the huts, I counted doors and shadows. The closest truck, the widest gap, the line of sight back to the trailer, little anchors to keep my nervous system from drifting. The ER had also taught me this: you don't have to be fearless; you only have to stay decision-capable.

Around us, groups laughed, traded phones for photos, and climbed into open-air trucks as diesel idled in a steady undertone. Voices rose and braided together. In all that bustle, I was the only one being pulled aside.

You're overreacting. I tried to breathe into that sentence. *You're tired. You're dragging old memories into a new moment.* I slowed my steps and checked what I could control again: receipt tucked where I could reach it, phone in my hand, bag cross-body. I glanced once at the line of trucks, then back to the man waiting for me. The distance between us was short and somehow still too long.

Normal was happening ten yards away and that contrast did strange things to time. A mother adjusted a child's hat and kissed the top of his head without looking a move so practiced it might have been a reflex. A teenager bargained for the outside seat and won, triumphant in the small way victories arrive at that age.

A guide swung the step down with a clack and said, "Watch your footing," the same way he'd already said it twenty times that morning. A couple argued gently about whether they'd locked the car and then decided to believe they had.

All those tiny predictable behaviors, the choreography of fun, made the path I was on feel narrower by comparison. If you were filming the morning, the camera would stay with the trucks, where faces turned toward vistas and the dust rose photogenically. No one would pan to the edge of the frame to catch the woman being peeled from the crowd by a man who didn't smile.

I used the normalness as a yardstick. If what was happening with me was fine, it should rhyme with what was happening there. Instructions, clipboards, light jokes about sunscreen. The rhyme never came.

Joe led me away from the cluster of people and toward a group of small huts near the trailhead. Even before we reached them, instinct clicked on. Exits, doorways, gaps between structures, the nearest vehicle I could step behind if I had to, I clocked them all. I tried to send a text in motion; the message spun and stalled.

Wind lifted dust across my boots again; a metal sign knocked lightly against a post. Behind me the rhythm of boarding went on, the life of the place undisturbed by the fact that my path had tilted.

At the threshold of the huts, I felt my body brace, nothing dramatic, just a steadying of weight into the balls of my feet, a readiness people mistake for calm.

I'll leave this chapter on the walk away from the crowd, because what came next belonged to another kind of story.

Chapter 7
The Waiting Game

He didn't lead me to the trucks with the others. Instead, Joe pulled me aside toward a cluster of small huts near the trailhead.

Up close, the huts felt older than the parking lot that hemmed them in dark, musty, the kind of structures that carry history in their walls. Narrow vents near the roof let in slits of light that striped the dirt floors. Even standing just outside, I felt removed from the chatter and bustle, as if a curtain had dropped between me and the rest of the morning.

Inside, the temperature dropped. The air had the coolness of shaded stone and the faint mineral smell of dry earth. Dust hung visible in the light shafts. The quiet pressed against my chest in a way sound never does. A thought arrived uninvited, flat and precise: *This could be the end of my life.*

"Mask in here," Joe said, touching his cheek. I pulled mine on, he never reached for one. The command felt less like policy than test. Heat pooled under the fabric; each inhale ricocheted at my mouth. I shifted forward, stance ready, keeping the threshold inside my peripheral vision and the distance to the door numbered in my head.

He began a low, memorized patter about how the huts were built and what they had been used for, lines delivered in a flat tone that sounded like a guide but did not land like a guide. Then, without transition, he pivoted to himself.

He told me about land his family owned, parcels without water, electric, or indoor toilets. He said these huts were the kind of shelters people built when the land was first settled. He said his wife had died, and his son, both in the same car accident, since then he had no one. The words were heavy with personal grief and completely out of place. I have that face, open, listening, the one that invites strangers to confess things they have never said out loud. Sometimes I joke and say I work for Gary's Shoes and Accessories for Today's Woman (which is where Al Bundy worked) just to deflect the oversharing. In the hut, I did not joke. I nodded once and let his story pass like weather.

He turned to me. "Want me to take your picture inside one?"

Harmless, on the surface. Normal, even. I hesitated, then handed him my phone with the camera already open.

He lifted it, frowned. "The screen changed. What's your password?"

He was no more than three feet away. His eyes stayed on the phone, but the question landed like a stone. Adrenaline washed through me so cleanly it felt like a temperature change. My breath rebounded hotter into the mask.

I smiled quickly and shook my head. "I don't know it," I said, already reaching to take the phone back. Face ID glanced at me and unlocked. The camera was still up, ready to shoot without any code at all. We both knew it.

The difference between a picture and a password is the difference between a moment and my life. I wasn't handing him entry to my messages, my photos, my location history, my bank apps; my everything.

I stepped so I could see both him and the doorway, receipt tucked where I could grab it, phone in my hand, bag strap across my body with the zipper in. He took two shots. The shutter's soft click sounded loud in the small room. When I look at those photos now my skin crawls. The sweatshirt I wore that day sits in the back of a drawer; putting it on feels like stepping back into the hut.

    We stepped into sunlight again, but the knot in my stomach tightened. Ten yards away, the tour kept happening on schedule, diesel rumbling, metal rails clanking, laughter lifting in little bursts. Families clustered for photos, couples held hands, groups scrambled into the open-air trucks with that buoyant, pre-adventure energy. It would have taken a single gesture to wave me into one of them. Even squeezing into a front seat would have been fine; I'd done that in Sedona when jeeps ran full. Instead, I was over here. Apart. It felt intentional.

From where we stood, the huts fell below the line of sight of the trailer and trucks. If you didn't know they existed, you wouldn't see them from the lot. We were roughly fifty feet from the nearest group, close enough to hear the laughter, far enough to be unseen. The air around the huts had that eerie charge you want to sage out of a room.

Joe stood beside me, silent now. His presence had weight. I checked my phone again, then again, hoping for the message that would make this separation make sense. Blank screen. No call. No text.

Breathe. Wait. Stay decision-capable. I repeated the words the way you steady a shaking bridge.

Without warning, he began to talk.

Chapter 8

The Interrogation

The silence stretched until Joe finally broke it.

He started with himself; his nationality, his background, words tumbling out in a rhythm that sounded half performance, half confession. Then he pivoted to the huts again, saying some were "male" and some "female," that this is what people built when the area was first settled. The cadence felt rehearsed, like lines said into a mirror until they stopped belonging to a person. His eyes never left mine. Unblinking. The longer they pinned me, the less I felt like a person; I felt like an object under inspection.

Then he turned the questions on me.

"What about you? What's your nationality? Were you born here? First generation?"
"Are you married?"
"Are you traveling alone? Why would you travel alone?"

He stood no more than three feet away. The air between us felt occupied, heavy. His tone mixed casual with interrogating, as if small talk were just the friendly mask of extraction.

I kept my answers clipped and bloodless. "Ohio." "Yes, I work." A nod where a sentence would normally go. None of it mattered. He didn't pause long enough to listen. The questions weren't for conversation. They were a list.

He shifted, gestured to his knee. "Surgery," he said, almost offhand then sharpened:

"Have you ever had surgery?"
"Do you have any medical issues?"
"Do you know your blood type?"

My stomach dropped. Those weren't tour-guide questions. They weren't even personal questions. They were clinical. Calculated. The kind you ask if you want to know what a body is worth.

Something in me moved from uneasy to certain with a single cue: his eyes. There was a vacancy in them that wasn't tiredness; it was distance. A detachment. I have seen it before in rooms where I used to work, the look of a person present and not present, intent and unconnected. In that instant the floor inside me tilted.

I tried to keep my face neutral, voice light, letting answers skim across the surface. Inside, I stepped out of myself. I felt the beat of my heart and the coldness moving into my hands, but my mind floated to a perch above the scene. Dissociation slid over me like glass: I could see, but I couldn't touch.

The sun beat down hard enough to flatten color. Heat bounced off the sand and climbed back through the soles of my boots. Somewhere behind us a truck revved and the sound passed through my body like a warning. I adjusted my stance so the light stayed at my back and the door to the huts remained inside my peripheral vision. If a body cannot run, it can still align.

And then a colder realization moved through me, slow and precise. His questions did not arrive from nowhere; they threaded through the days that had led me here:

- The strange phone call two nights earlier, the woman asking three times if I was a "single traveler."
- The official company that never called back, never answered my messages.
- The woman in the trailer who somehow knew I'd been waiting for another tour, though I had not said it.

The pieces clicked together with the clarity of glass breaking. I was not unlucky. This was not a harmless mix-up. It was orchestrated. And the plan had reached me.

He asked the question he wanted most. "Why are you traveling alone?"

This time I didn't answer. Couldn't. My tongue weighted itself; my gaze fixed past his shoulder, unblinking like his had been. Silence thickened until it pulsed in my ears with my heartbeat. For a breath or two I thought, *This is it. This is the last sound I'll ever hear.*

Maybe I was reading into everything. My phone had been useless, my room wasn't ready, and the day had already rubbed me the wrong way. I told myself it was the perfect recipe for paranoia. I had watched forty or fifty people climb into open-air trucks smiling. The simplest explanation, I reminded myself, was that I was tired, not that anything was wrong.

"Joe, it's ready."

A woman's voice cut the air, too clean, too rehearsed.

I turned. The woman from the trailer was striding toward us with an economy of motion that read like protocol. Her steps didn't waver. Her face didn't search mine. She didn't even look at me when she added, "**She's ready.**"

The spell broke, but not with relief. Air rushed back into my lungs and brought something heavier with it: confirmation. Joe wasn't improvising. He wasn't alone. She was part of it.

The sun pressed hotter. The world narrowed to angles: hut, trailer, trucks, the thin rectangle of shadow at my feet. I understood, with a clarity that left no room for argument: I was no longer just in danger. I was inside something designed.

Chapter 9

The Van

When the woman called out, "Joe, it's ready. She's ready," a flicker of hope rose in me. Maybe I'd finally join one of the open-air trucks I'd watched all afternoon, benches, chatter, cameras, safety in numbers.

That wasn't where Joe led me.

He guided me to a plain grey van parked off to the side. The windows were heavily tinted, the kind that reflect the sky back at you and open only a few inches at the bottom. Glass meant to hide what was inside.

I climbed into the first row. The vinyl was cold; it caught faintly at the back of my jacket. The air was stale, diesel threaded with dust, the sour tang of old upholstery. An older woman, **the grandmother**, sat directly behind me. In the back row, a younger woman balanced a baby in her lap. A toddler drifted between them, curious and restless. At one point she climbed forward and showed me her newly painted nails, small fingers held up for approval.

On the surface, the tableau should have reassured me: a family, a baby, a toddler. Normal.

It didn't feel normal.

The grandmother was silent, presence heavy and wordless. The younger woman leaned toward her and whispered in a language I didn't recognize. The words came low and quick, urgent, never in English. Once or twice the grandmother's eyes flicked to me, brief, unreadable, then away. I could not tell if they were warning each other or warning me, if they were with me or with *this*.

Outside, Joe lingered by the driver's door. He leaned in and asked for proof of payment. I handed him the small handwritten slip the woman had given me.

He took it and then shook his head. "No, the other one. The paper that shows you're allowed to be on the land. It's probably in your car."

My chest tightened.

Before I could argue, he started the engine and rolled the van across the lot, stopping nose-to-nose with my rental. For a heartbeat I tasted escape, open the door, slide into my car, drive. But he had angled the van so his body blocked the driver's side. I would have had to push past him. Every instinct screamed **run**; logic kept me still.

I did as I was told. I opened my door, shuffled papers, lifted the one he wanted. I kept my voice even as I handed it over. He glanced, tossed it aside with no interest. I retrieved it and tucked it into my hiking bag.

Later I would see it: he never needed that paper. Sending me back to my car let him mark it. Now he knew exactly which vehicle was mine.

The van eased away from my car and headed for the exit. My chest cinched. Why were we leaving? The tour should have begun at the trailhead; the trails were right there. Joe said, almost casually, "We just need to get gas."

I tried to do the math the way a tired ranger once taught me: distance, time, fuel, margin. Stations out here live where roads cross; they do not hide beside trailheads. If we truly needed gas, he would have filled **before** taking passengers or sent us to wait at the trailer while he topped off alone. Ninety minutes doesn't require a detour, unless the plan is not ninety minutes.

I traced the road signs through the tint the way you read a stranger's face in a dark bar: for shape, not detail. A speed limit that didn't match the park roads. A mileage sign to a town I knew was in the opposite direction of the overlook I had circled on a map. We passed a picnic pullout I recognized from my drive in, only now we were approaching it from the wrong side. Small proofs, one after another, that the story I was being told did not rhyme with the landscape I knew.

Tours I've taken start with choreography: head counts, names, a safety speech, the joke the driver keeps sharpened. Here there was only engine, heat, and a van that sealed itself like a container. I pictured the open-air trucks still loading beside the trailer, that obvious stage where anyone can wave if they need help, and felt the distance harden between *what should be* and *where I am*.

I pressed my shoulder blades into the seat and let the pressure anchor me. Panic makes tunnels; pressure makes edges. Edges help you think.

It didn't add up. Stations were miles away; this was only a ninety-minute tour. Unease spread through me like ice while the van carried us farther from where we should have been.

The tinted glass made it worse. The bright desert blurred into a darker mirror; my reflection floated faint and ghostlike, as if I were already vanishing. If I screamed, would anyone know I was here?

Inside smelled like old vinyl and the faint metallic sweetness of hot coolant. The A/C coughed once, blew lukewarm, and quit. The toddler's shampoo, berries, cut through the diesel every time she leaned forward. Sun seamed light along the window gasket and slid across my thigh in a slow stripe. Somewhere behind the dash a panel rattled at a pitch I could feel in my molars.

I gave myself a loop to run so my mind wouldn't run me: breathe in for four; count what is real; breathe out for six. Real: seat belt latched; door handle visible; my bag strap looped across my body with the zipper facing in. Real: grandmother's shoe tapping a soft, steady rhythm; baby's fist opening and closing around a corner of blanket; driver's hat brim cutting the windshield into two hard angles.

The reflection in the glass showed me doubled, a ghosted version layered over desert, with the toddler's bright hand lifting through both worlds to display her nails again. "Pretty," I said, and made my voice ordinary. Ordinary tones are tools.

My phone lay in my lap, screen glowing. I began the ritual: type, send, wait. Signal bars appeared and disappeared, sometimes SOS mode, like a cruel magic trick. Most messages failed. I tried again.

One went through.

I'm on a tour and feel nervous cause this driver seems drunk.

It was the safest phrasing I could find, light on the surface, heavy underneath: *something is wrong.*

Another message slipped out:

His name is Joe, and he said he's taking us to get gas.

I sent my location, a pin on the map. A breadcrumb. Proof. I hoped it had gone through.

I took screenshots of each message the moment I sent it. It's a reflex from the ER: document while you can, because later you may not be able to retrieve what mattered. **2:41 p.m.** driver seems drunk. **2:42 p.m.** his name is Joe; says he's getting gas. Location pin sent at **2:42** and **2:43** in case one lagged. **2:43 p.m.** I'm scared. The words looked small on the screen; the time stamps looked large. I let the numbers steady me the way a monitor steadies a room, cold, impartial proof that moments existed.

I drafted one more text and sat on it for a count of twenty:

If you don't hear from me by 5:00 p.m., call the hotel and then call the police.

I didn't send it, half because I didn't want to frighten the person on the other end, half because saying it would make a private fear public. Instead, I saved it to Notes where my thumb could find it fast. Prepared does not always mean pressed "send."

I tilted the phone so the glass didn't flash; I didn't want to draw attention. In the front corner of the screen, bars continued to rise and fall like a tide. When they rose, I pushed a message through. When they fell, I wrote the next thing I would say for the second the tide turned.

At **2:43 p.m.**, a fourth message reached out:

I'm scared. The guy told us his wife and child were killed in '95 and now he has no one.

My hands trembled; sweat dampened my palms. A metallic taste edged my tongue. My body locked into the seat while my mind leapt from terror to contingency and back again. I added the detail about the women, how they whispered in a language I couldn't understand but the tour driver could. At first, I suspected they were part of it. Every silence became a reason to be afraid.

Only the toddler cut through. She drifted between rows, tugged at her mother's sleeve, showed me her nails again, her small voice a counterpoint to the engine's low hum. A flicker of innocence in the middle of a tightening room.

Another message finally reached someone I trusted, not enough to make me safe, but enough to keep me breathing. I fixed on that fact the way a climber fixes on a single hold.

We kept driving, past the lot, past the trailhead, into distance. Six miles. Seven. Maybe eight. I lost count. The sun hammered the roof, heat rose from the road in visible waves.

Then came the sign you celebrate on vacation and dread when your gut has already decided: **a state line.** For most tourists it would be a joke: *Another state!* For me it felt like a trapdoor opening. Another layer of distance. Another way to disappear.

Crossing a state line on a map is a thin stroke; crossing it in a van feels like a threshold. The welcome sign is meant to be festive; new rules, new sky, same sun but I felt the border like a hinge in the day: before, after. Jurisdictions change here. So do response times, radio channels, and the way people give directions. If someone later asked, *Where were you?* I would have to answer, *It depends when you mean.*

I marked the crossing in my head the way you notch a tree on a hike so you can find your way back. I noted the color of the sign, the shape of the post, the texture of the shoulder where gravel gave way to sand. These are the kinds of details people don't think they'll need until they need them. My breath steadied a little. I moved my heel half an inch so I could feel the floor through my boot. Bodies remember paths even when minds fog. I intended to give mine one.

    I stared through the tint, phone clutched tight in my lap, willing another message to break through.

Chapter 10
The Warning

The van glided onto a pristine concrete lot, no gravel, no traffic, under a bright LED canopy. This wasn't a dusty roadside relic; it was immaculate. Fresh concrete poured in broad, uncracked slabs, the kind that makes tires whisper. A modern LED canopy washed everything in clean light. The storefront gleamed, glass without hard-water haze, brushed-metal door pulls, planters with actual landscaping instead of plastic buckets. It had the quiet confidence of **money and order**, well kept, recently updated, control in the details.

We rolled to the first pump just inside the entrance, from a bird's-eye view, the right-rear pump of the island. The lot was nearly empty: just us and a white, windowless van idling across the way with its rear doors open. No passing traffic on the road, none on the way down, either. The stillness read as curated rather than neglected, like a stage between scenes. A light wind moved across the concrete and brought only the cleanest trace of gasoline, the kind of place where spills are mopped before they dry.

"Go ahead and get out, browse while I fill up. Won't take long," he said, almost casual, almost friendly.

My hand was already on the door handle. The plan was clear: step out, circle behind, snap the plate. A breadcrumb, proof I'd promised myself I would leave. I had even texted the plan earlier, a warning disguised as routine: If I disappear, here's the trail.

I had rehearsed this in other cities, little rituals that make a woman visible to the right people and invisible to the wrong ones.

A plate photo. A quick pan of the lot. A text with time, direction, color, shoes. Women pass these methods to one another the way divers pass air.

No one formally teaches you; you learn because you've been followed once, or because a friend has, or because your grandmother pressed her lips thin when you were thirteen and said, If something feels wrong, leave the feeling and keep your body. Even now, my body moved ahead of sense, already making evidence of itself. I didn't yet understand that sometimes a hand around your wrist can be a gift.

Before I could move, fingers clamped around my hand.

The grandmother leaned forward, grip like iron. Her eyes were sharp, unflinching. When she spoke, the words were meant only for me.

"**Don't move,**" she whispered. Her breath brushed my ear. "**See that van? They're going to snatch us.**"

I froze.

Language can be a siren or a scalpel. The way she said it left no room for the kind of doubt that tries on optimism like a shirt:

Maybe this is nothing. Maybe they're waiting for someone else. Maybe I'm being dramatic. Her whisper sliced those maybes clean off.

The men across the lot did not perform guilt. They performed patience. They stood the way fences stand, already placed, already purposeful.

A grin would have been easier to dismiss. Patience is harder; it says we have all afternoon to become the ending you don't want.

Across the lot sat another van, plain and windowless, back doors yawning open like a mouth. Three men stood near it, boots planted, hats pulled low, sunglasses hiding the eyes. They didn't fidget. Didn't lean. Didn't pretend to be busy. They stood the way people do when waiting is the job.

Up close they read as average build, work-day uniform: jeans, boots, white shirts, the kind of cowboy hats that shade a face into anonymity. Their white van sat with its back doors open, no side windows, a posture that suggested arrival rather than errand. The cool metal of my door handle pressed into my sweaty palm; the mismatch of temperature and skin made the moment feel hyperreal. Somewhere under the canopy the pump nozzle clicked against its holster, an absent, repetitive sound that said fueling without proving anything was flowing. The road beyond the lot stayed vacant, a long ribbon of nothing moving. In a city you can disappear into crowds; out here, you can disappear into silence.

I glanced sideways and caught Joe looking at them too, not idly, but watching.

My heart lurched into my throat. My legs stayed rooted to the floorboard; my chest cinched until each breath felt like pulling air through a straw. I tasted metal.

Over 1,500 miles away, at 3:11 p.m. Mountain time, my mom lifted her phone and typed: Are you okay? I wouldn't see it until later, but the timestamp chills me still. While I sat in a grey van staring at a white van with its mouth open, my mother's instinct crossed the miles like a flare. I have looked at that timestamp more times than I can forgive. I have thought about the submarine cable that carried my mother's impulse, the satellites like glitter in the daylight, the towers that put a ladder under a single text and brought it to my phone.

The world is a net and sometimes it holds. I don't think of this as luck. I think of it as the physics of love, an equation where alarm travels faster than sound.

Inside, the grandmother leaned closer. Her grip softened; her voice sharpened.

"I'll tell him we're late for a wedding reception," she murmured. "My uncle's waiting. If I point to the motel up the hill, he'll believe it. People are expecting us."

It wasn't a lie; it was strategy. Not just buying time, planting consequence. We cannot vanish without notice.

I took in the station fast, like a medic scanning a scene. Three other pumps. A glass-fronted store with posters sun-bleached from the inside. A convex mirror over the door. As we idled, a lone sedan rolled to the far pump, the driver topping off, gaze fixed on the numbers like they were sentences; a woman in a visor worked the ice chest by the doorway, back turned. Trash can, blue windshield squeegee, a rubber mat by the threshold. Camera domes dark under the canopy, real or props, impossible to tell. The open van with the men sat just beyond the edge of the concrete apron; from there they could watch every door, every angle.

Joe reappeared in the doorway, resting a forearm against the frame. His tone was light, almost playful, but there was glass under it.

"Aren't you going to get out and browse? This pump's taking forever."

I didn't turn. "I'm good," I said, aiming for bored, not scared. Ordinary tones are tools.

The grandmother squeezed once, a signal. The younger woman caught my eye in the rearview tint and gave the smallest shake of her head. The toddler hummed to herself, tapping her new nails against the vinyl, pink, pink, pink like a metronome for courage.

Joe shifted his weight. The pump clicked; the handle didn't thump back into its cradle. He hadn't actually started fueling. He was staging.

The choreography became visible once she named it. Open doors. Idle engine. A driver who asks you to step into the light and turn your back.

You can teach yourself to see it the way you can teach yourself to read an EKG, pattern first, then consequence. I thought of my family, my clients, anyone who might hear this someday and say, But how would I know? This is how. Stillness that looks like waiting. Questions that inventory a body.

Kindness that arrives as an order. A story that pins you to your seat by pretending to be small talk.

The grandmother moved first. She leaned toward the open driver-side window, voice pitched practical and annoyed, the cadence of a relative herding a late driver.

"We're late," she said. "We told my uncle we'd be at the reception already." She pointed up the road. "At the motel. Right there."

The words carried the shape of logistics, nouns you can check, places you can verify, a clock someone else owns. I watched his face for the half-second of calculation. People who intend to take you like it when you have no appointments.

"We'll be quick," he said. "Just—" His eyes slid to the open, windowless van across the lot, then back. "—a minute."

She didn't blink. "He's waiting. We have to go now."

Silence held, taut as wire. The three men by the other van didn't move.

I said nothing. Fear wanted me to fill the air. Training, mine and hers, said do not negotiate with your safety.

He exhaled through his nose and flicked his chin toward the driver's seat. "Fine."

Her fingers released my hand. For a heartbeat we sat in the dense quiet that follows a decision. The open van across the lot stayed a mouth.

She whispered, so low I felt it more than heard it: "When we stop, we get out. Together."

Chapter 11

The Return

The grandmother didn't hesitate. She straightened, met his eyes, and delivered the line like she'd been preparing for it all her life.

"**Jim,** we need to get back now. I can't miss this wedding; my uncle is waiting."

Jim.

It was the first time I'd heard her call him that. He answered without flinching, as if the name fit. Nothing about him felt fixed. Later I would wonder how many names he wore, how many masks he kept ready for strangers who never saw the danger underneath.

Names are levers. In hospitals, names link charts to bodies; in small towns, names link bodies to families. He answered to **Jim** as if he had practiced the reflex, no lag, no glance to the woman at the window to confirm the alias. It was the smoothness that troubled me, not the name itself. Smoothness means rehearsal. Rehearsal means a pattern. I pictured a drawer of name tags in some unseen back room, Jim for tourists, Joseph for paperwork, another for nights when paperwork is a problem. The more a person can be called, the harder they are to find.

Suspicion cut across his face. "Who's your uncle?"

She didn't blink. She gave him a name, firm, steady, deliberate, the kind you remember. It carried weight, the way certain names do in places where kin is currency. It said: someone will notice if I vanish.

Some names travel with a shadow. You feel the outline even if you don't know the story. The one she chose landed with weight.

I watched him measure it, a mental scale tipping between bravado and caution. Power is rarely about volume; it's about who believes you belong to someone who will come looking.

"We're already late," she pressed. "We still need pictures before the reception."

His jaw locked. He muttered something in his own language, clipped, sharp. She answered in kind, tone perfectly matched, refusing the inch he tried to take. Their words collided in the air, fast, hot, unrelenting. I did not have the language but I recognized the grammar, call and answer, advance and block, the old music of a woman refusing to be moved.

Even the toddler felt it, her play going quiet as if her small body understood that the adults were building a bridge we would have to run across.

I watched the exchange the way you watch a fuse burn, counting instinctively, measuring what's left. He tried to crowd the space with statements; she answered with facts: time, place, the name again, a reason photos mattered. When he leaned in, she reclaimed inches by pointing, out the door, up the road, turning his body to look where she wanted him to look. It was subtle, almost polite, but effective: a choreography of redirect.

My own body mirrored her choices. I widened my stance a fraction, flattened my hands on my knees to keep them from shaking, and let her voice carry. If he needed a reaction, he would not get mine; if he needed agreement, he would miss it while he calculated hers. The pump's screen threw pale light across his jaw; the nozzle hung idle though the clock ticked, time passing with nothing to show for it. When he finally yanked the handle, the metal clanged the way anger sounds when it has to be small.

He grunted, frustrated. With a violent motion he yanked the nozzle then slammed the handle back. The tank wasn't full; he hadn't even pumped a penny of gas. He didn't care. He cared about control, and Glorietta (the name I had given her in my head) had just taken some of it.

Only then did I register the scale of what she'd done. The grip on my hand, the lie, the insistence, those choices were keeping us alive.

He slid into the driver's seat and his gaze cut toward me, probing again. His voice came smooth, almost casual, a blade wrapped in cloth. More questions, another attempt to draw me into his web.

Glorietta moved first. She leaned forward, voice light, almost cheerful. "So, where are you from? Do you like the snow?"

Vanilla questions. On the surface harmless; in practice a shield. She built a wall of ordinary talk between me and him so I could breathe and answer in fragments without inviting more.

My replies were thin, "Ohio." "Yes, I work." but her steadiness wrapped around us like armor.

I made myself small without looking small, shoulders back, chin neutral, hands folded where I could see them. Breath in for four; hold for four; out for six. On the out-breath I counted real things to keep the room from tilting: belt latched; door handle visible; bag strap across my body with the zipper turned inward. The heater pushed air that smelled faintly of vinyl and coolant; the toddler's berry shampoo cut through every time she leaned forward. The grandmother's knee touched the back of my seat in a steady rhythm, not fidgeting, a metronome.

I watched the mirror so I didn't have to watch him. The mirror gave me angles without eye contact: the set of his jaw; the way his hat brim cut the windshield into two hard panes; the quick, checking glances he threw left and right as if expecting confirmation from a place I could not see. I had the sudden thought that people like this wear identities the way mechanics wear gloves, pull on, pull off, discard when thin.

I rehearsed the only three sentences I would allow myself, should he press again: *I don't have that information. I need to check with my family. Please take us back to the trailhead now.* I smoothed them flat in my head like cue cards, short, repeatable, nothing to embellish. When panic asked for more words, I told it no. Words are doors; I would not open more than three.

The van rattled back toward the trailhead. Through the tint I saw him raise his hand in a small, precise motion.

A signal.

Across the lot the other van's rear doors slammed shut. The crack hit my chest. No license plate, just an empty frame.

Cold moved through me.

By the time the trailhead came into view, my hands shook in my lap. Then color: bright dresses, dark suits, laughter lifting into open air.

A wedding party stood near the trail, posing for photos.

There are coincidences that feel like mercy. The dresses moved like flags; the photographer's hands lifted and dropped in commands; someone laughed from the belly. Joy spilled into the space like water, filling every crack where danger liked to hide.

Later, when memory tried to argue that maybe it wasn't that bad, I would recall the way his eyes skated over the color and decided, quietly, privately, not today.

Even through the tint you could feel the brightness, fabric that caught the sun, shoes that hadn't found dust yet, the staged awkwardness of people about to be remembered. The photographer lifted a hand and the group rearranged, everyone turning by instinct toward instructions. Nothing attracts attention like a camera pointed outward; nothing deters secrecy like a camera pointed everywhere.

I tracked the angles automatically: if we stopped here, any door that opened faced faces; any sudden movement would be framed in a dozen candid shots. I thought of how photos time-stamp truth, who was present, which vehicle, what the sky looked like. For once the calculation favored me. He saw it too. The van slowed that imperceptible amount that means a decision has already been made and the body is only now obeying it.

My hands wouldn't steady. I tucked them under my thighs so the shake wouldn't show and fixed my eyes on the line where asphalt met packed dirt, the line I would cross when told to go.

My chest tightened. *We still need pictures before the reception*; her lie had materialized in front of us as if the world had decided to corroborate it. Too many witnesses. Too much attention. Light where shadows require dark.

He slowed. He didn't comment. He didn't have to.

The photographer lifted a hand and the group reset again, half-turns, dresses swished, boutonnieres adjusted. For once, the physics of attention bent toward safety.

I tracked the practicals because practicals keep a body decision-capable: distance from our bumper to the edge of the lot; the slope where asphalt gave way to packed dirt; the angle that would put the wedding party between me and him if I needed to move. My palms were slick; I dried them on my jeans, then laced my fingers to hide the shake. The toddler hummed again, three bright notes that didn't know what they were interrupting.

When the van rolled to a stop, sound changed. Engines fall silent a fraction before a brain trusts they have; in that fraction, relief arrives like heat lightning, visible, not yet useful. I felt it crack across my chest and refused to follow it out of the moment. **Doors first. Feet next. Then decisions.** The cool air hit like a correction, clean, mineral, almost sweet. The kind you feel in your teeth.

I stepped down and placed my body where my shadow fell toward the wedding party. The grandmother came even with my shoulder, not behind it. We looked like ordinary people pausing to orient, which is the safest costume an endangered person can wear. Her eyes flicked once to the left, check, confirm, and the set of her jaw told me what the words would be before I heard them.

"**When I say go, you run.**"

Chapter 12
The Escape

The van doors slid open and my legs decided before the rest of me did. I ran.

Cold air cut my throat. Light hit like a flash. The lot stretched bright and merciless, and the world blurred into blocks of glare and shadow. I aimed not at people, not at buildings, just at **distance**. Concrete gave way to the darker strip of asphalt and then the raised lip of the sidewalk. I climbed onto that narrow, man-made ridge as if it were higher ground.

Only there, on the line where parking lot meets road, did sound return. The flag across the way snapped once. Far behind glass a bell chimed. Somewhere metal clicked, pump handle, holster, an empty sound that said *fueling* without proving anything flowed. My sunglasses went on so the tears could do their work unseen.

I ran straight, all the way to the sidewalk near the picnic table where I had sat earlier. Distance became a moral choice. The farther I could get from the van, the more I believed in the possibility of breath.

My lungs burned hot, metallic, and my legs shook as if they'd been asked to carry an extra body. Maybe they had, my future self, heavier with survival.

When I turned, she was already there.

Glorietta stood at the open trunk of her car, squared and steady, as if she had been waiting for me to choose her out of the whole scene. No wave. No fuss. Just eyes fixed on mine, the look people use when they are hauling you back into your body.

"Listen to me."

Not loud. Not frantic. **Authoritative**. Her tone cut through adrenaline the way a shoreline cuts through surf.

"Leave now, while it's still light," she said. "Drive **six** over the limit. Not more." Her gaze didn't let me look away. "Do **not** stop. Not for gas, not for food, not for the restroom. If you have to stop, it's somewhere loud and crowded, McDonald's, Walmart, never quiet."

I nodded because language felt far away and nodding was the piece I could still reach.

"If someone follows too close," she went on, "don't slow down and don't wave them around. Keep going until you hit the interstate. Even police cars, don't pull over on an empty road."

She stepped closer, took both my hands in hers, the same firm, unyielding grip she'd used in the van, and lowered her voice so it belonged only to us.

"They use bait," she said. "Dogs. An old man on the shoulder. A woman with a baby. Anything that makes kind people stop. That's how they rob them. Sometimes that's how they **snatch** them."

My hands shook inside hers. The tremor had borders now; the shaking belonged to a body that knew what to do next.

I believed her because my body already had.

Then she told me why she knew.

Her niece had lived through it.

The way she shifted, shoulders square, voice low, told me this part had a cost. Some stories you tell and hand back to the air.

Some you tear from your own skin and place in another person's palms so they will understand what you mean when you say this is not a myth.

"She was dropping off some of the handmade items we made and needed to use the restroom. She thought she was safe," Glorietta said. "Locked the door on one of those portable toilets." A pause. "Then it **shook**."

Her fingers tightened over mine. My breath stalled.

"They wrapped it shut from the outside, bungee cords, tight. Before she could scream, the whole thing lifted."

"She dropped her phone into the waste," Glorietta said. "No calling out. No way to text. Just her and her mind."

The picture hit me full force: darkness fused with chemical blue; plastic walls flexing with each breath; the sway of a truck bed; a phone slipping from slick fingers into the waste where help goes to drown.

I saw it the way the nervous system makes movies: her niece rocking the box side to side, throwing shoulders against the door, counting under her breath because counting proves time still exists.

"She thought like a river," Glorietta said. "If a thing can be lifted, it can be dropped. She threw her weight side to side until the straps complained. She aimed for a rut. She told herself, *Break. Break. Break.*"

Glorietta's voice stayed controlled, a practiced line that wouldn't let itself break. Her eyes did not waver.

"It worked. They hit something or she found it. The box spat itself from the truck. The latch split. She ran like a fire moving uphill."

Silence pooled between us.

"She hid in a storage hut, wood and dust, no light. She put her ear to the ground because sound carries there. She did not yell for anyone because there was no yelling left to do." Glorietta swallowed. "A cousin found her hours later, shaking so fast her teeth made a sound. She came home alive."

"What happened after?" I asked, though I already knew after is where the price is counted.

The word alive landed like a metal weight on soft ground

Survival recalibrates a household. Locks are not metaphors; lights are not ambience; noise is not nuisance; it is proof that other bodies are near.

Safety becomes a communal choreography: somebody always home, somebody else driving, doors that answer when you check them.

Freedom shrinks to a room you can see all four corners of, and you teach yourself to be grateful for square footage that used to feel small.

"But nothing was the same," she continued. "My boyfriend does the deliveries now. My daughter doesn't drive alone. My granddaughters are never left with their father. We keep the house full, lights on, doors locked, working toilets. That is safety now. That is what it costs."

Her gaze flicked past me, toward the portion of lot where the grey van we had been in had been waiting. The air between us felt charged the way air feels before weather changes.

She told me this wasn't a spontaneous outing; it was a trial run they'd built like a bridge, plank by plank. For years they had lived on the property the way people live inside a locked room, by routine, by watchfulness, by making the perimeter small enough to manage.

This day was the first time Glorietta, her daughter, and her granddaughters had left together without the men who usually shadow their movements. They had circled the date on a calendar. They had rehearsed the route. They packed snacks and extra water like they were packing nerve. 'Just one day,' she said. 'See the mountains. Take pictures. Prove to the girls the world can be ordinary.' Then, quieter:

'Without my uncle. Without my boyfriend. To see if we can be like other people for a few hours.' She looked past me toward the lot, the vans, the cameras, the wedding, and her mouth set. 'We are safe at home because we do not move. Today was to test moving.

The statement set a weight between us: her risk, my survival, balanced and visible.

Hope is reckless and necessary. You take children to the mountains because you want them to remember that the world has high places, that their lives are not confined to hallways and errands. You gamble a day. You hold your breath in a van. You make a story out of caution and call it adventure because sometimes that is the only way to carry your people into sunlight.

She squeezed my hands once more; a seal pressed into wax. "**Go.**"

Chapter 13

The Escape Instructions & Drive

We stood at her open trunk, her hands anchoring mine. The metal edge pressed a line into my palms; it felt like a guardrail at the lip of a drop.

"You need to leave **now**, while it's still light." Her cadence was practiced care, not panic. Each word arrived clipped and usable, like tools laid out in a row.

She repeated again: "Drive **six miles over** the limit, six, not more. Do **not** stop on this land. No gas. No food. No restroom. If you absolutely must stop, it has to be **crowded**, McDonald's, Walmart, a place with noise and eyes. If someone follows, you do not wave them around and you do not slow down. Eyes forward. Hold your speed. Stay with the plan until you hit the **interstate**."

She spoke in the grammar of logistics because calm can hide inside nouns: interstate, Walmart, light, crowds.

I felt the steadiness of it settle into my bones. When panic wants poetry, survival wants instructions.

I felt her certainty settle into my body the way a seatbelt does, tight, uncomfortable, unmistakably designed to keep bones in one piece.

Then she told me the part that still chills me.

"They would have sold the **babies** to people looking to adopt. They would have sold my **daughter** into prostitution. And you and I" she held my gaze, as if she could pin me to the truth "they would have taken our **organs**, the ones that would sell, and left us at a trailhead. Dead."

There are sentences you cannot hold and keep breathing. I broke them into parts, taken, trailhead, left, and swallowed each with water from a bottle I didn't remember opening.

I thought of headlines that make women into warnings. I thought of the way strangers say Don't hike alone as if a sentence could reverse a map.

The air thinned. Heat flushed and drained from my face. She kept going because protection, here, meant naming the thing completely.

"They make it look clean on paper. Your rental left somewhere hikers leave rentals. A few card charges to write a false path. A text to your family that says you're fine. And then silence. Weeks later, animals erase what matters. The file reads, *woman hiked alone and made a mistake*. The truth never enters the case."

My brain tried to minimize it, *unlikely*, *dramatic*, because minimizing is the cheapest form of comfort. The counterargument arrived like a gavel: **this kind of harm depends on your doubt.** The thought clicked into place inside my chest, the sound of a lock engaging.

I nodded. My throat felt raw. Sunglasses hid the tears that still found their way out.

She squeezed once, steady, not soothing. "**Go.**"

I turned toward my car and then turned back, pulled by the only words big enough for the moment. I stepped into her space and **hugged** her, hard, brief, the way you hold a life preserver. "Thank you," I said into her shoulder, into the smell of dust and laundry soap. "I'll pray for you and your family every day."

I had never prayed outside a childhood picture-frame verse. The sentence surprised me; the truth of it did not. She nodded, eyes soft and fierce at once, as if she understood both the promise and its weight.

I walked to my rental. The keys were uncooperative in my shaking hands; twice I missed the slot. Inside, I locked the doors, pressed the metal until the latch thunked, and set the key in the ignition.

And **froze**.

Late-afternoon light pooled across the dash, warm and indifferent. Bargaining began its litany: *Maybe you're overreacting. Maybe check in at the hotel. Maybe the wedding means you misread it. Maybe she is reacting to her own history.* Beneath the spin was something solid: **she knows**. I had seen the knowing in her eyes, the kind people carry after survival rearranges the furniture of their lives.

Two habits arrived like muscle memory. First, the quick **inventory** I teach and too rarely use: doors locked; engine off but ready; bag angled where my hand could close on the strap; keys accessible; line of sight to the exit; first turn planned. Second, breathing with numbers because numbers obey when feelings won't: four in, four hold, six out, until my hands belonged to me again.

Signal stuttered back to life. I typed with thumbs that still trembled, sending the story in **fragments** to three people, small, survivable pieces of the truth:

I was on a van tour.
Something felt wrong.
She saved us.
I'm scared.

The bubbles came and stalled and came again, that jagged rhythm of desert coverage. Replies landed like lights switching on in separate rooms of the same house:

No. You're not overreacting. Leave.

We're here. Text until you say you're safe.

Get to the interstate.

My decision hardened. I said it aloud to make it contractual with myself: **"Four hundred dollars isn't worth my life."**

Money had been the scaffolding for my week, tickets and rooms and gas, small proofs that I could buy myself days of quiet.

Now it felt like a joke told at the wrong time. The math was this: four hundred dollars is a number. A body is not.

I signed the equation with my foot on the brake.

I started the car. The engine note felt too loud. Tires whispered over clean concrete as I eased from the space and out onto the road.

Every nerve retuned itself to the **mirrors**. Rearview. Left. Right. Any shape behind me read as intention. A pickup merged a quarter mile back; my heart climbed to my throat. I set the cruise to **six over**, exactly as instructed, and still watched the needle because I trusted my hands more than the machine.

Glorietta's sentences looped like scripture:

Don't stop.
Don't wave them around.
Don't slow down.
Drive faster.

Rules prevented terror from freelancing. I made a cycle for my eyes, mirror, road, shoulder, instruments, repeat. The landscape widened and emptied in the same breath. I named what was **actually** there so I wouldn't invent ghosts: *gate,* *arroyo, mile marker, ocotillo, cattle guard.* Then I named the feeling anyway: *afraid, but moving.*

Only then did I let out a sound I hadn't realized I was holding in, something between a breath and a sob. I pressed the phone's side button without taking my eyes off the lane and said, "Text sent," so the people on the other end would know I was moving, and that the word *safe* was getting closer, one mile at a time.

Chapter 14

The Aftermath

The road to the interstate felt endless, **one hundred eighty-five miles** that stretched like pulled taffy. Distance lost its ordinary math. A mile could take a minute or an hour; time seemed to slow down on purpose so I would have longer to be afraid.

The sun stayed high and unapologetic. Its brightness didn't soothe; it **sharpened**. Shadows cut black seams at the bases of the buttes. Glass glittered in a turnout like teeth. Fence posts leaned with their splinters pointing toward the road as if to mark me passing. Heat made a fine electrical sound, a quiet buzzing I heard more in my bones than my ears. Even the horizon looked alert, as if it had been assigned to watch.

I drove in **silence**. No music, no talk radio, not even weather.

Silence can be a helmet or a hallway. Today it was both. I wore it to keep the noise out and walked it to get from now to next.
The hum of tires became my music: mile, mile, mile.

I could not spare a single word for anything that wasn't *lane, mirror, shoulder.* The tires hummed their thin, relentless note and I let it become a metronome: breathe on the count, check the mirror on the count, keep going on the count. My breaths rasped too loud cloth over mouth, air rationed.

Signal toyed with me. Bars rose and vanished, the phone face a tide chart I could not read. Each time I thumbed my mother's number the call fell through the floor. Texts spun in place, blue then green then failed. With every failure my chest added weight without adding space, like sandbags stacked where lungs should be. *What if I'm already gone to everyone but me?*

Everything on the shoulder read like a **trap**. A dog trotting too close to the white line, pausing, looking back, exactly the kind of bait Glorietta had named. I tightened my hands and did not brake. An abandoned shack listed under the heat; the doorway yawned dark enough to imagine a man waiting just inside. I made myself inventory **facts** so I would not invent ghosts: mile marker 114; a green cattle guard sign; ocotillo bending in the wind; one hawk circling.

Then the imagination argued back: headlights slamming into the rearview, a truck nosing my bumper, metal folding, hands on my elbows dragging me across gravel, the van's doors closing like a mouth. I could feel dirt under fingernails that weren't yet dirty. The mind will supply evidence for any terror it is asked to carry.

I started snapping photos without looking, console, dashboard edge, the smear of my shaking hands on the wheel, a slant of sky. Click, click, click. Useless pictures on purpose: breadcrumbs. If the world swallowed me, someone might scroll the camera roll and see the direction fear points when it tries to leave a trail.

The crying arrived like weather changes: sudden wind, then thunder. Heat first, then the flood. My throat burned raw, my chest hitching against the belt. The steering wheel quivered under my grip; I could feel my pulse in the leather. I tried to breathe like I teach, four in, four hold, six out, and sometimes the numbers caught and sometimes the numbers blew away like dust.

A **single bar** of service blinked alive. The phone vibrated like a small, trapped animal. With hands that felt underlined in red pencil, I dialed.

"Mom—" The word came out broken. "I—there was a van—a white van—I—" The sentence would not line up. She didn't ask me to be coherent. She used the kind of voice you press onto a wound. "It's okay. You're okay. You're safe now." She said it more than once so I could stand inside it.

When the call dropped, I looked at the screen and saw a **message** I hadn't seen, green bubble landed hours earlier: **3:11 p.m. MT**. At that exact minute I had been rigid in the van's first row, watching three men in hats stand by a white van with its doors yawning open. My mother had typed **Are you okay?** and thrown it into the desert like a flare anyway. The timestamp hit harder than anything else. It felt like a seam had opened in the day and her instinct had threaded a line through it to catch me.

A semi settled into my lane a quarter mile ahead, its trailer flexing as if shrugging at the wind. I kept my **six miles over**, not five, not seven, exactly as I was told. Rules were armor: *Don't stop. Don't wave them around. Don't slow down. Keep going to the interstate.* I said them out loud until the sentences sounded like they had existed before I did and I was simply obeying something older than me.

I performed the cycle: mirror, road, shoulder, instruments, repeat. Name what is real: flashing yellow for a school turnoff; the long silver of a cattle truck; a crest, a dip, a length of asphalt bleached to pewter. When panic tried to freelance, I assigned it tasks: count the fence posts to the next mile marker; check that your bag is where your hand expects; draft what you would say to 911 if you had to talk in code.

The desert did its big trick, endless and claustrophobic at the same time. Sky pressed down like a lid, and still there was too much of it. Every vehicle was suspect. A white van idled on the shoulder, nose outward as if pointed already at me. A pickup hovered in the rearview glass longer than I wanted and then slid back, innocent or not, impossible to prove. A police SUV sat in the cut of a side road, windows black, unreadable. Glorietta's warning replayed verbatim: *Even police cars. Sometimes a dog. Sometimes an old man. Don't stop.*

Sweat crept from my hairline. My palms slicked; I wiped one hand on my hiking pants and regripped. I realized my jaw ached; I'd been holding my teeth together like a door against wind. I told my face to soften and it did not listen.

The urge to pull over arrived in respectable disguises: *Prove you're fine. Get your bearings. Text where the signal is strong; it will only take a minute.* Each time the no rose from my chest like a reflex, same tone Glorietta used: *Do not stop on this land.* Obedience is a kind of shelter.

Mile after mile, the road held. The sun shifted, its light slanting into hard angles across the hood. Somewhere a radio tower blinked and disappeared again. I passed a billboard for a gemstone shop with an arrow pointing down a road I did not take. A man stood at a mailbox in the middle of nowhere, flipping envelopes with the slow patience of someone who belongs to a place; I felt like a ghost passing him.

Another sliver of service. A reply slid through from a friend: **We're with you. Keep driving. Text when you hit the interstate.** I let it sit unread at the top of the screen because looking down wasn't on the list of permitted movements. Instead, I counted guardrails. I rehearsed the parking-lot choreography I would use if I had to pull into someplace fluorescent and ask a cashier, calmly, *Could you call security to walk me in?*

Time went watery. The odometer clicked; I believed it because numbers are less likely to lie than feelings. The car carried my shaking without judgment. My fear kept trying to narrate an ending and I kept offering it tasks.

Finally, green rising out of heat shimmer, the **INTERSTATE** sign. Block letters that look the same in every state, a font that feels federally guaranteed. Relief didn't arrive all at once; it came in increments, like light working up a wall. I said the word out loud so my body would hear it: "Interstate."

Hope has a way of knocking before it opens the door. I did not answer. I kept my eyes on the lane and let it find its own key.

I planned the merge like a lesson: signal early, check mirrors, check again, leave space you can live in, don't overcorrect. I held **six over** through the arc and settled into the right lane. I refused the rearview for ten slow counts, because safety sometimes means **not** looking where fear wants you to. When I finally glanced up it showed only road and sky, no open mouth of a van, no hat-brim silhouettes, just distance, which for the first time all day felt like something I owned.

Town gathered itself from the horizon: low rectangles, a water tower, the corporate geometry of signs. My body did not trust it yet. I opened the hotel app with clumsy thumbs and booked a room, any room, just to nail the day to a place with a door I could lock.

The small act steadied me the way pressing your palm to your sternum steady's dizziness.

In the lot I cut the engine and the sudden quiet collapsed onto me like a roof. Adrenaline drained fast; my hands shook with the aftershocks. Skin too thin, bones too heavy. Relief braided with dread until I couldn't separate them. I let my forehead rest on the heel of my hand and listened to the tick of cooling engine metal, a small domestic sound that felt like permission to keep existing.

The phone **buzzed**. **Voicemail.** Timestamp: **2:52 p.m.**

At 2:52 p.m. I had already been driven away in a white van, sending ragged texts through static. I pressed play.

Her voice was light, almost cheerful. The **tour operator who had called the day before**. She said she'd been **officiating a wedding** earlier and had told her drivers to expect me for the **11:00 a.m.** tour. Since I "hadn't shown up," she assumed I wasn't coming.

I watched my own reflection in the black screen as if the glass could argue on my behalf. I had told her **three times** I would not arrive until **midday**.

The voicemail arrived like a script delivered too late to change the scene: cheerful tone, false detail, the neatness of 11 a.m. sewn over the hole where I should have been.

It was the kind of plausible that might comfort a person who didn't want to know better. I had learned better. The neatness was the tell.

In the quiet car, the pieces **locked**, not like an idea, like a mechanism finishing its cycle. The neat false detail. The pleasant tone. The timing. It didn't sound like confusion. It sounded like a **cover story** already lacquered and ready for any official ear that might come asking.

If anyone had asked, the file would read clean: *She was scheduled for 11. She didn't show. Case closed.*

I put the phone face-down on my thigh and watched my hands tremble against the fabric.

I had made it out.

And the truth lodged where breath should go, bright and unshakable:

I was supposed to be gone.

Chapter 15

The Telling

I sat in the car outside the hotel until the engine ticked itself cool and the dashboard clock changed twice. Forward felt theoretical. The lot was quiet, the kind of evening quiet that makes a person audible to herself, and I could hear the shallow, stubborn rhythm of my own breathing. Normally I would bypass the lobby entirely: digital key, elevator, door, lights. A clean seam between outside and in. Tonight, the app flickered *error* and held its ground. If I wanted a room, I would have to cross the threshold like a person who needed help.

Sunglasses stayed on, not because it was bright but because my eyes were not ready to be seen. I walked in as if the air were thicker indoors, as if moving through it required proof of effort. The clerk glanced up and did not interrogate my face. No cheerful *How are you?*, no petty bureaucracy. "We've upgraded you," they said, already sliding a key card across the counter, already setting two cold waters and a small arrangement of snacks where my hand would find them. Kindness practiced as policy. It landed the way a blanket does, neither cure nor explanation, simply warmth.

Kindness is a shock. It makes your eyes sting worse than fear does. I nodded too many times because I did not know how to hold the relief of being seen without being consumed.

Food was an argument I did not want. My body felt hollowed and overfull at once, fragile and untethered, the way a balloon looks after the knot slips. Still, I knew the math: salt and protein anchor a person; a meal convinces the nervous system that the world will continue. In the lot a low-lit restaurant sat a hundred, maybe two hundred steps away. A laughable distance most nights. Tonight, a mountain.

The glass doors exhaled cool air as I stepped out. I told my legs *just to the curb,* and then, having made it that far, *just to the painted stripe,* then *just to the lamppost where insects spun like confetti in the cone of light.* Every few paces my body tried to bargain me back into the lobby. I answered with the oldest medicine I know: one step, then the next, then the next. I carried Danny tucked in my bag. To anyone else, perhaps ridiculous. To me, a talisman: proof I could still choose a small, light thing and take it with me.

I have learned not to apologize for what steadies me. Ritual is not childish; it is engineered. The body responds to objects the way a skittish horse responds to a familiar hand.
Touch, breathe, okay. Try again.

At the host stand I asked for a table where I could see the door. My phone buzzed, one of my people offering to stay with me the whole meal, voice or text, whatever I could carry. *Please,* I wrote back. *Talk me through it.* We kept a thread open, a lifeline that hummed across the table between the water glass and the untouched menu. I ate slowly, mechanically at first, then with a little more belief. Grease, salt, temperature, ordinary sensations auditioning to become appetite.

I have a lifelong skill for pretending to be fine. That night I let the pretense rest. I let the cracks show. My friends, family in everything but DNA, poured steadiness into the spaces where steadiness had leaked out. No grand speeches. Just consistency: *I'm here. Keep breathing. You're safe in this minute.* Words like armor, fitted quietly at the joints.

Somewhere between the entrée and the second glass of water, the room softened. The clatter of dishes resounded like proof that life continued in other people's hands. A child laughed three tables over; a server apologized to a couple for a forgotten side and fixed it; ice settled in a pitcher. Nothing cinematic, just the ordinary choreography of a place where nothing bad was happening. Gratitude arrived not as a feeling but as a comprehension: these are my people; this is my net; this is how I am carried.

When I stood to leave, the night had cooled. The walk back across the lot was measured on purpose. Each step felt heavy and deliberate, like placing stones to rebuild a path I might want to use again. The lamppost released its cloud of insects; the painted stripe shone faintly; the hotel's glass doors opened as if I had been expected. I crossed the lobby, passed the arrangement of armchairs where no one sat, and held the key card to the reader.

The lock answered with a clean, mechanical click, sharp, final, steady. Hours earlier I had listened to van doors slam like punctuation at the end of a threat. This sound was the opposite. It meant *mine*. It meant *inside*. It meant that for tonight, in this square of light with my name on the folio and my shoes toe-out by the door, survival was not a concept but a room.

Chapter 16

Silence & Transformation

In the days that followed, I began saying it out loud. Saying it out loud kept the silence from colonizing everything. Silence is not empty; it is mold. It grows in the dark and softens the structure if you let it. Story is the sunlight. I aired the rooms carefully, window by window, person by person, until the smell lifted.

Not to everyone, only to the circle that knows my real voice when it shakes. Family. The friends who answer on the first ring. People who have stood in my kitchen and seen me laugh with my whole face. I told the story in sections, like lowering a heavy thing to the floor without breaking it. Each time a voice held steady on the phone, each time a message glowed back *I'm here*, I felt a small stitch tug skin to skin. Language can be a suture if you let it.

There was one person I did not tell.

My grandmother has always worried me from airport to airport, her questions soft and relentless: *Do you have snacks? Are you wearing good shoes? Text me when you land.* Now she was fighting cancer with the quiet stubbornness that built our family, and I could not set this weight on her lap. She didn't need to carry my almost. Protecting her meant carrying the silence myself. It is strange how silence weighs more than words; you lift it all day without anyone seeing the strain.

Something in me re-arranged after that day, like furniture moved in the dark and the room never returned to its old shape. The brush with what almost happened took a blade to my life and left the edges clean. I saw what belonged and what didn't.

I let go of people who lived on my battery like a background app, always open, always draining. No speeches. Just a new math: if the cost is peace, the answer is no. Boundaries that once felt like meanness turned out to be oxygen. I learned the sentence that ends arguments and explains nothing: **That doesn't work for me.** I said it gently and often. The sky did not fall.

At the same time, I leaned harder toward what is mine. My family. My chosen family. The group chat that chirps everyday logistics, photos of soups, screenshots of weather, the exact shade of the sky at 7:14 p.m., and then, when needed, holds a heart the way both hands hold water. Ordinary moments put on weight: a Tuesday dinner, a shared cart through a fluorescent aisle, a dumb joke that refuses to stop being funny. The mundane became sacred because I understood how fast a life can be **interrupted**.

And always, Glorietta walked with me. Her hands around mine, warm, dry, decisive. The quiet of her voice in my ear: *Six miles over. Do not stop on this land.* The way she cut panic into numbers and turned a parking lot into a plan. Her courage braided into mine like a second set of lungs. When I tightened my grip on the wheel weeks later, it was her steadiness I was holding.

I promised her I would pray for her family every day. Up to then, prayer had been a framed bedtime rhyme from childhood, nice words with no hinge. After, prayer became a task with a job: say the names, keep them lit. I am not a theologian. I am a woman who whispers a stranger's name in the kitchen while the kettle shudders and believes the sound crosses a distance.

This is not only a story about almost being trafficked; that word is too flat for how the ground moved. It is a story about **survival** and **reassignment**, of attention, of allegiance, of time. One day drew a line through my life and labeled the sides **before** and **after**.

After means I live differently. With clarity that doesn't apologize. With courage that isn't loud but refuses to move. With intention measured in small proofs: fuel at half tank, routes with exits, yes to the people who steady me, no to what costs too much. After means I keep telling the truth, even when my voice shakes, because telling it keeps me from being swallowed by the silence that tried to take me.

Epilogue

Choosing Life

When I think back to that day, it still feels like a story I walked into by accident and had to write my way out of. A tour that should have been ninety quiet minutes almost became an ending. A stranger's hand, warm, dry, decisive, closed over mine, and a whisper cut the spell. That is the seam where my life did not divide.

The fear still lives in my body like weather. I carry the clean brightness of the gas-station canopy; the open, waiting mouth of the white van; three men who knew how to hold still; the way a phone can display *Sending...* long enough to feel like betrayal. I remember the highway through tears; miles blurred into one sound: tires insisting forward. None of that leaves. But neither does this: I am still here.

This is not only a story about "trafficking." The word is too flat for how the ground moved. Exploitation rarely looks like the poster; it is administrative. It hides in laminated menus and cheerful voicemails, in cash-only windows and questions that should never be asked on a tour, *Are you alone? What's your blood type?* It preys on our kindness, our habit of smoothing edges, our urge to be agreeable. It prefers witnesses who aren't looking yet.

And still, there are counterweights within reach. Instinct is evidence. Documentation is protection. Crowded places are strategy, not cowardice. You are allowed to leave, to say no, to refuse to explain your refusal. You are allowed to survive out loud.

I think about sounds: the slam of van doors hours before; the clean click of a hotel lock later that night. One was a threat with punctuation. The other was a sentence I got to finish. I keep both in mind when I measure what a day is worth.

So, I will keep living the "after" with clarity that doesn't apologize, courage that doesn't need volume, and gratitude sturdy enough for weekdays. I will keep saying her name. I will keep choosing the crowded place, the documented plan, the voice that does not shake even when my hands do. Survival is not modest; it demands a life that answers back.

If survival is a beginning, what begins for you today?

Resources & Safety

If you or someone you know is in immediate danger, call your local emergency number.

- **U.S.:** 911 • **U.K. & EU:** 112 (also 999 in the U.K.) • **Canada:** 911

Crisis Hotlines (24/7, confidential):

- **U.S.:** National Human Trafficking Hotline – 1-888-373-7888 (text BEFREE to 233733) • humantraffickinghotline.org
- **Canada:** 1-833-900-1010 • canadianhumantraffickinghotline.ca
- **U.K.:** 08000 121 700 • modernslaveryhelpline.org
- **U.S.:** RAINN (sexual assault) 800-656-4673 • rainn.org
- **U.S.:** National DV Hotline 800-799-SAFE • thehotline.org
- **988 Suicide & Crisis Lifeline (U.S.):** Call/text 988

For international hotlines, see **lastradainternational.org** or **findahelpline.com**.

Numbers and websites can change; check current details before travel. This page offers information, not legal advice. Your awareness, and willingness to act safely, can interrupt harm.

Stay Connected

- Free checklists & reading guide: **tenaciouscle.com/resources**
- Newsletter (occasional): **tenaciouscle.com/newsletter**
- Speaking & Workshops: traveler safety • boundaries • bystander action • book talks **info@tenaciouscle.com**
- Clinical practice (non-urgent): **https://tenaciouscle.clientsecure.me**
- Media & permissions: **info@tenaciouscle.com**| Instagram **@tenaciouscle** | LinkedIn **www.linkedin.com/in/sara-unger-malpcc-s**

For emergencies, please use the crisis resources listed in the previous section; I cannot respond to urgent messages via email or social media.

Professional Disclaimer

This book reflects my personal experience and professional opinion and is educational, not a substitute for individualized mental-health, legal, or safety advice. If you need clinical care, please contact a licensed provider in your state or call/text **988** (U.S.) for immediate support.

Afterword

When I replay those hours, I still hear door, one that opened to risk, and another that closed to safety. This book is my way of keeping the second door open for someone else. If you are reading this because something similar happened to you, please know: you are not alone, and you are not to blame. If you are reading because you love a traveler, student, or friend, thank you. Awareness isn't fear; it's freedom with better tools.

    I am grateful to the people who taught me what to look for, who answered late-night calls, and who believed me. Most of all, I am grateful to Glorietta, whose presence and clarity changed my outcome. May this story travel farther than I did that day, and meet you exactly where you need it.

Acknowledgments

To the woman I call **Glorietta**, and to her family: I carry your names every day. Your steadiness changed the ending of my story, and I will honor that as long as I have pages.

To my **mom,** whose instinct crossed a thousand miles at exactly 3:11 p.m., you are the net I fall into and the reason I climb back out.

To my **grandma**: I hope you know how much I miss you. Your gentle questions, your stubborn love, and your way of making ordinary days feel special live inside these pages with me.

To my bestie **Eric** for texting with me while I ate dinner that evening. I can always count on you.

To my family, chosen family and friends: thank you for answering on the first ring, for sitting with me in the messy middle, for laughing me back to myself, and for reminding me to eat.

To the readers, librarians, booksellers, and book-club leaders who place stories into hands: you help the right words find the right people at the right time.

To solitary travelers everywhere: may your rituals keep you, may your instincts speak up, and may you return with more of yourself.

Notes & Further Reading

The following organizations and books informed my understanding of trafficking, traveler safety, and bystander response. If you'd like to learn more, these are good places to start:

- Polaris Project: National Human Trafficking Hotline (U.S.) and research briefs.
- La Strada International: European network on human trafficking.
- International Organization for Migration (IOM): Counter-trafficking and assistance programs.
- UNODC (United Nations Office on Drugs and Crime) : Global reports on trafficking in persons.
- U.S. Department of State: *Trafficking in Persons Report* (annual).
- U.K. Modern Slavery & Exploitation Helpline: guidance and statistics.
- RAINN and the National Domestic Violence Hotline: survivor-centered support.
- Harriet C. & Kevin Bales, *Understanding Global Slavery* (introductory overview).

(Website addresses change; search by organization name.)

Reading Group & Classroom Questions

Preface

These questions are meant to guide reflection and dialogue. They invite readers to consider both the personal and systemic dimensions of safety, risk, and resilience. My story is one perspective; your discussion may bring out insights I never imagined. Use these prompts to deepen understanding, connect experiences, and explore ways to build safer communities.

Book Club Questions (personal, reflective)

1. What moment in the story most shifted your understanding of risk or safety? Why?
2. Which warning signs seemed obvious only in hindsight? Which were visible in the moment?
3. How did naming *Glorietta* shape your experience of the narrative and of gratitude?
4. What part of the story stayed with you most strongly: fear, relief, gratitude, or something else?
5. How did the author's survival shape your view of resilience, faith, or intuition?
6. If you were to share one takeaway from this memoir with a friend, what would it be?

Classroom Questions (practical, applied)

1. How can language or cultural differences complicate seeking help or being understood, even within the U.S.?
2. Where is the line between vigilance and hypervigilance for travelers? How do you maintain it?
3. What bystander actions in the story felt realistic? What else could have helped?
4. If you designed a five-minute safety briefing for students or travelers, what would you include?
5. What systems (transport, lodging, online platforms) could change small processes to reduce risk?
6. How can we talk about trafficking and exploitation without stereotyping places or communities?
7. After reading, what will you do differently in your daily life or next trip?

About the Author

Sara Unger, MA, LPCC-S, LPN is a licensed mental health therapist whose work bridges clinical practice and prevention. In her private practice in Ohio, she helps clients heal through trauma-informed, strengths-based care, drawing from CBT, ACT, MBT. She is the author of several practical workbooks, among them *So, You're Navigating ADHD, Now What?* and *So, You're A Teen, Now What?* used by individuals, groups, and community programs.

This book recounts her near-trafficking experience from a traveler's point of view and the bystander whose courage changed the outcome. Today she delivers keynote talks that translate that day into practical tools, situational awareness, healthy boundaries, and compassionate bystander action, for schools, workplaces, and community groups.

Resources, media kit, and speaking: **tenaciouscle.com**. Clinical inquiries: **https://tenaciouscle.clientsecure.me**

How to Use & Share This Book

You may quote brief passages for reviews, education, and discussion with proper attribution. For speaking requests, classroom use, bulk orders, or permissions, contact info@tenaciouscle.com